WHAT DOES IT MEAN?

WHAT DOES IT MEAN?

Bible Culture Revealed

---

by Michael A. Verdicchio

Library of Congress Cataloging-in-Publication Data
ISBN: 1729718469
EAN: 978-1-7297-1846-9

Dedicated to my two grandchildren, Ava and Betsy Rose, and any future grandchildren.

Thank You

I am thankful beyond measure and beyond words to our loving God for allowing me to learn some of His matchless Word as well as the privilege of sharing His Word with others.

I will be forever grateful to my wife, Kathy, who has been by my side for 47 years; she is a faithful companion, a virtuous woman, and my best friend.

I have tremendous gratitude for those through the years who have taught me great truths from God's Word.

I am thankful to those who have and are supporting my ministry – may God bless you abundantly.

And, a special note of thanks to Michelle Armstrong and Carli Morris who edited this book. Their expertise and labor of love was instrumental in helping me to present this material with simplicity and clarity. Thanks to Angela lamb for assisting with some of the formatting.

Table of Contents

Preface

I have been an avid student of the Bible for over 40 years. As an ordained Christian minister with the great privilege of teaching God's Word, I still consider myself a student of the Scriptures. I continue to search God's Word for added light and understanding.

I was first introduced to eastern customs in the Bible during a biblical class in 1975. A portion of the class was devoted to keys of how to get a proper interpretation of the Scriptures from the Scriptures themselves. One of the keys discussed was orientalisms.

I live in the western world. The people of biblical times lived in the eastern world, or what we refer to today as the Middle East. Thus, the Bible is indeed an eastern book.

The word "orientalism" communicates to me, and it may to others as well. However, I decided not to use that word in the title of this book, being mindful of those not familiar with that word or this topic. *What Does it Mean?* explains various verses containing manners, customs, and idioms of the times in which the Bible was written as well as some figures of speech (in addition to idioms) divinely employed in the Bible.

Over the years I have thrilled at the added understanding of many verses once I understood the culture of the Bible. I have studied many resources concerning this topic and taken numerous biblical classes and lectures where various orientalisms were shared.

By far, the greatest resource for me has been the teachings of Bishop K.C. Pillai. In the late 1970's, I enjoyed reading three of his books. Later, I had access to many, many more of his teachings, both printed and audio recordings. While I am deeply grateful for all the biblical classes and teachers I've learned from for over forty years, in my opinion, Bishop Pillai is the foremost authority on this topic, period.

Let me explain why.

Bishop Pillai was born in 1900 in India and raised Hindu. When he converted to Christianity, his family disowned him, literally holding a funeral service and burying his picture in a casket. Nevertheless, he was ordained a bishop in the Eastern Orthodox Church in India. Later, he would be sent on a special mission.

At the time of the Bishop's early life, his native India had remained an isolated country for thousands of years. Therefore, the customs and manners of the people were still aligned with the eastern, biblical culture. Much of the rich eastern culture and tradition Bishop Pillai was reared and educated in has changed dramatically. The twentieth century saw great changes around the world, which eventually included India. Bishop Pillai's knowledge of eastern culture brought great understanding of the Scriptures to the western world.

Sir S. Radhakrishnam wrote, "Any interpretation of the Jewish religion which ignores the total environment in which it grew up would be dangerously narrow."[1] Add to that the words of Max Muller, "Whatever sphere of the human mind you may select for your special study, whether it be language, or religion, or mythology, or philosophy, whether it be the laws or customs, primitive art or primitive science, everywhere, you have to go to India, whether you like it or not because some of the most valuable and most instructive material in the history of man are treasured in India, and in India only."[2]

Bishop Pillai once wrote, "The Oriental traditions and philosophy are foreign to the Occidental world in general. Therefore, it is essential that one understand the Oriental thought and way of life (especially that of India, since the culture of India was adopted by the Middle East and Near East centuries before the birth of Christ). Otherwise, one will be unable to understand the Spiritual significance of the Scripture. We cannot believe what we do not understand."[3]

---

1   Sarvepalli Radhakrishnan, *Eastern Religions and Western Thought* (Oxford University Press 2007), 23
2   Max F. Muller, *What Can It Teach Us* (Book Tree 1999), 37
3   Bishop K.C. Pillai, *Orientalisms of the Bible* (Mor-Mac Publishing Company, Inc. 1969), xii

Recognizing the lack of understanding in the western world, the Indian Orthodox Church sent Bishop Pillai on a mission: to bring the light of the Scriptures through understanding the culture in which it was written. Bishop Pillai spent the last twenty years of his life acquainting Christians with the orientalisms of the Bible, imparting great enlightenment of the eastern culture. His mission carried him to numerous universities and seminaries as well as every major denomination throughout Europe, England, the United States, and Canada.

In *What Does it Mean?* the reader will gain an understanding of many verses as well as some practical application for consideration. An understanding of what a word or phrase means can be very enlightening and inspiring. However, the practical application presented will also be of great benefit to the reader.

This book is not a re-presentation of Bishop Pillai's writings or teachings. Rather, it is a culmination of my study and understanding of the Scriptures.

It is my sincere hope and desire that *What Does it Mean?* adds clarity and understanding of the Scriptures to the end one can readily apply that understanding in his or her daily life. And, should a reader feel like, "a bottle in the smoke," I pray he or she can allow God's Word to be, "a lamp unto thy feet," and thus be, "renewed like the eagle."

Introduction

Unless otherwise noted, the chapters in this book were originally published as articles on my blog, Confidence and Joy. Some chapter titles and articles have been re-formatted and re-edited for this book. Each chapter focuses on a specific word or phrase from a verse in the Bible (KJV). You will discover a clearer understanding of that verse from the insight given regarding the culture of biblical times with respect to manners, customs, idioms, and other figures of speech.

For example, what was the intended meaning when the psalmist wrote, "I am become like a bottle in the smoke?"[4] One might readily recognize the figure of speech employed in that verse, but what exactly was "a bottle in the smoke?"

The same is true in reverse. Perhaps there are people in parts of the world that would not understand if they read something in a book that said, "He threw some dogs on the grill." Here in the United States one would easily understand, but those in another part of the world may be a bit puzzled and wonder what kind of "dogs," why they were thrown, and what a "grill" is? They lack understanding of our culture and idioms.

In addition to understanding idioms relating to the culture of the Bible, understanding figures of speech are also helpful. There are three figures of comparison that are not only quite common in the Bible but also used often by people today.

The first is simile, which is a comparison by resemblance usually using "like" or "as." If a person is a really good swimmer, someone might say, "He swims like a fish." Psalm 1:3 says a righteous person is "like a tree planted by the rivers of water."

The second figure is a metaphor, adding more emphasis than a stated comparison. A metaphor is a comparison by representation where one noun or pronoun represents another. In the fish example above,

4   See Chapter 1

a metaphor would be, "He is a fish." In John 15:5, Jesus said to his disciples, "I am the vine; ye are the branches..."

Adding still more emphasis and intensity is the figure hypocatastasis, which is a comparison by implication. In the fish example, instead of comparing the swimmer with a fish by saying he is like a fish, or even that he is a fish, in hypocatastasis the comparison is just implied. "Look at that fish!" Although the comparison is implied, the meaning is effectively communicated.

In John 10:10, Jesus did not say the devil is like a thief; he did not say the devil is a thief; he said, "The thief cometh not, but for to steal, and to kill, and to destroy: I am come that they might have life, and that they might have it more abundantly." He put some very serious emphasis on his statement.

Whether it's hypocatastasis, metaphor, or simile, these figures are used widely throughout the Bible. When we recognize them and understand the biblical culture, the meaning of many verses is unlocked. A great resource for understanding figures of speech is *Figures of Speech Used in the Bible* by E. W. Bullinger.[5]

You will also read some practical application of an explained word or phrase. Other verses relating to the subject under consideration referenced in a chapter are printed at the end of the chapter.

Whether you just love reading the Bible, you are an avid student of the Bible, or you are a teacher of the Bible, your heart will thrill as the meaning to dozens of verses becomes clear.

All Scriptures referenced in this book are from KJV unless otherwise noted.

---

5   E.W. Bullinger, *Figures of Speech Used in the Bible* (reprinted 1968 Baker Book House Company), 123

How to Use This Book

Reading the whole book: Simply reading this book cover to cover will be an exciting adventure in learning more of God's Word by understanding many manners, customs, idioms, and other figures of speech employed in the Bible.

Table of Contents: The title of each chapter in most cases is taken from the verse itself. Looking through the table of contents, you may recognize phrases from familiar verses in the Bible (KJV). Reading each specific chapter will provide insight and a much greater understanding of those specific verses. As such, each individual chapter provides a great resource for those who teach the Bible.

Chapter 1

A Bottle in the Smoke

For I am become like a bottle in the smoke;
yet do I not forget thy statutes. Psalm 119:83

I remember the first time I saw an empty soda bottle in a campfire. Someone had tossed it in to see what the hot coals would do to it. We watched over time as the shape of that glass bottle changed.

The memory of that campfire event was the first thing that came to mind when I read the above verse about a bottle in the smoke. Of course, I quickly realized in biblical times they didn't have glass soda bottles, so I was a bit puzzled by what a bottle in the smoke could possibly mean.

In biblical times, poor people who did not have a well of their own would keep a supply of water in a goatskin. Once skinned and cleaned, they would tie the four legs with rope, pour fresh water in, and tie the neck with rope. They would then hang it on a pole.

Many people lived in a small, one-room dwelling. This is where they would sleep, cook, and eat. As a result from cooking, the bottle (goatskin) would hang there, subject to smoke and heat. Over time it would become charred, crack, and leak, becoming useless. In that culture, if one was to tell someone he or she was like a bottle in the smoke, this would be easily understood.

The bottle in the smoke cannot control the unpleasant circumstances that surrounds it; it is alone and helpless. At times in life we may feel this way like the psalmist did, but he went on to say, "Yet do I not forget thy statutes."

Remembering the "statutes" means the psalmist did not forget God's promises, written or declared. There are other words used in the Bible synonymous with what God has declared: precepts, law, commandments, testimonies, judgements, etc. Despite his seemingly hopeless and helpless situation, the psalmist knew deliverance from God was available; he did not forget His statutes.

When we face times of discouragement or crisis with seemingly no help, when we feel alone, hopeless, and helpless, we can remember where our help comes from. We can remember His promises of deliverance. We can look to God, rely on God, and trust in our ever-delivering, and all-powerful God!

———————————

Psalm 119:83
For I am become like a bottle in the smoke; yet do I not forget thy statutes.

Chapter 2

He Made Bare His Holy Arm

The LORD hath made bare his holy arm in the eyes of all the nations;
and all the ends of the earth shall see the salvation of our God.
Isaiah 52:10

In our modern times, it is unheard of for kings, presidents, or prime ministers to be present on the battlefield. However, in the lands and times of the Bible, it was commonplace for kings to not only be present but also fight in the battles. This custom was carried out well into the Middle Ages.

In the Bible there are many accounts of kings fighting in battles. Some were successful, and some were not. Keeping in mind kings did indeed fight in battles helps us to understand the meaning of God bearing His holy arm.

The robes of kings in biblical times were long garments with long sleeves. In times of battle, the king would remove his robe. The sleeves would be tied together in a knot. The knotted robe would be put over his head so that his robe would then be behind him, held by the knotted portion that was around his neck.

This indicated to all those present as well as to the enemy that the king was not hindered in any way. His arms were free and unobstructed. He was prepared to fight.

There are places in the Bible that talk about God's arms, but does God literally have arms? No. Scripture tells us God is spirit. Giving God humanlike characteristics is the figure of speech, anthropopatheia. It is "the ascribing of human attributes, etc., to God."[6] Utilizing this figure gives great emphasis to God's strength and power.

---

6   E.W. Bullinger, *Figures of Speech Used in the Bible* (reprinted 1968 Baker Book House Company), 871

Arms are a symbol of strength. One can read about God promising to deliver the children of Israel out of Egypt with a "stretched out arm," showing God's great power and might to do such a thing. This is much more emphatic than to simply say, "I will deliver you."

God making bare His holy arm is not only indicative of His strength and power but also of His willingness. He has removed His robe. He is ready to go to work. He is ready and willing to fight for His people.

We might have more confidence in God when we call upon Him for help if we remember that He indeed does bare His arm for us today as well. Sadly, some people do not feel worthy of God helping them in such a dramatic fashion. They think, "Oh, maybe a little bit of help, but certainly not taking off His robe and going to battle on my account. Who am I that He should do something like that for me?"

Would a parent hesitate to help his or her child? I certainly would not. The Bible declares we are children of God. That is either just a nice religious phrase or it is literally true. It is true. We are His children, and nothing can separate us from His love.

Since there are numerous places in the Scriptures that encourage us to call upon God for help, why shouldn't we expect that as a loving Father, He would indeed help us? Perhaps instead of looking at our weaknesses and shortcomings, we ought to put our focus on our powerful and delivering God!

Why not picture Him taking His robe off and bearing His arms for His children, not because we are worthy, not because we have earned it, but simply because He loves us.

––––––––––––––––

Isaiah 52:10
The LORD hath made bare his holy arm in the eyes of all the nations; and all the ends of the earth shall see the salvation of our God.

Exodus 6:6
Wherefore say unto the children of Israel, I am the LORD, and I will bring you out from under the burdens of the Egyptians, and I will rid

you out of their bondage, and I will redeem you with a stretched out arm, and with great judgments:

Deuteronomy 33:27 (NIV)
The eternal God is your refuge, and underneath are the everlasting arms. He will drive out your enemy before you.

John 4:24
God is a Spirit: and they that worship him must worship him in spirit and in truth.

Galatians 3:26
For ye are all the children of God by faith in Christ Jesus.

Romans 8:38 and 39
For I am persuaded, that neither death, nor life, nor angels, nor principalities, nor powers, nor things present, nor things to come,

Nor height, nor depth, nor any other creature, shall be able to separate us from the love of God, which is in Christ Jesus our Lord.

Chapter 3

The Ox Knows His Owner

The ox knoweth his owner, and the ass his master's crib:
but Israel doth not know, my people doth not consider. Isaiah 1:3

There is an expression some use today when referring to someone who is not very smart. They say that person is as dumb as an ox. I do not know if oxen are stupid or not, but in this verse in Isaiah God is clearly implying His people are not as smart as an ox - or an ass!

In small villages in the lands and times of the Bible, early in the morning a young boy would lead the animals out to the fields. He would go to each master's home and lead the animals to the field to graze. He would lead the asses from their cribs and the cows and oxen from their mangers.

In the evening the young boy would not bring the animals back to each owner's crib or manger. Instead, he would simply bring them back to the edge of the village and let them go. The cows, asses, and oxen would find their way to their own master's crib or manger.

Apparently, those animals were not so dumb after all. The asses knew where their masters' cribs were, and the oxen knew where their masters' mangers were located. They had the sense to return home.

God was saying, rather bluntly, His own people had forgotten who their Master was. They did not even have the sense of an ass or an ox. The ass and ox knew where their masters were, but Israel did not know or even consider their master. Those "dumb" animals knew where their masters were, but God's own people did not.

Using something they were familiar with, God was very pointedly showing them that they really ought to remember who God was and how He could provide for them. If they would have remembered that, then they would not have needed to go chasing after other gods, putting their trust elsewhere, instead of trusting in God.

Understanding the culture of the Bible, one can easily see this verse in Isaiah is a blistering statement of reproof. God was telling His people that they did not even have the sense of an ass or an ox.

God will provide for those who put their trust in Him. He provides solutions, liberty, peace, joy, healing, and abundance - all that we need. For those who are not even as smart as an ox or an ass who choose to return back to God, He will indeed provide for them as they put their trust in Him.

Isaiah 1:3
The ox knoweth his owner, and the ass his master's crib: but Israel doth not know, my people doth not consider.

Philippians 4:19
But my God shall supply all your need according to his riches in glory by Christ Jesus.

Malachi 3:7
Even from the days of your fathers ye are gone away from mine ordinances, and have not kept them. Return unto me, and I will return unto you, says the LORD of hosts.

Chapter 4

Walk in the Light of Your Fire and Sparks

Behold, all ye that kindle a fire, that compass yourselves about with sparks: walk in the light of your fire, and in the sparks that ye have kindled. This shall ye have of mine hand; ye shall lie down in sorrow.
Isaiah 50:11

This verse in Isaiah speaks of those walking in the light of their own sparks. In the lands and times of the Bible, farmers did not live on the farm; rather, they lived in the village. Thus, they would rise very early in the morning to work at their farms.

Around 4a.m. at the time of the first cock crowing, those going to work in the fields would rise. A fire in the village would be lit, and many would gather to warm themselves before heading out. They would then walk barefoot in the dark, often along very narrow paths.

In order to have some light, they would light the end of a piece of rope at the village fire. Then they would blow on the rope producing a small shower of sparks. This provided a little bit of light for them until they reached the fields.

In Isaiah 50:11, it talks about walking in the sparks, walking in the light of one's fire, resulting in sorrow. To those living in that culture, the meaning was very clear - rejecting the light of God's Word and walking in one's own light will produce sorrow.

On the other hand, Psalm 119:105 speaks about God's Word being a lamp unto one's feet, and a light unto one's path. In the dark, is it better to walk by the light of sparks or a lamp?

Many people get discouraged and defeated in life, and as it says in Isaiah, they are laying down in sorrow. Why? They try to walk by the light of their own sparks, but our own sparks are not enough.

It reminds me of Jeremiah 2:13 regarding God's people forsaking Him, the fountain of living waters, and instead choosing broken cisterns. A fountain has an unlimited supply, whereas a cistern is limited, and a broken cistern is pretty much empty.

People have free will to choose, but when they forsake God's wisdom they will be disappointed. Isn't it better to rely on a fountain instead of a broken cistern?

Our own light and our own wisdom always come up short compared to the light and wisdom of God. The best we can do compared to God is sparks, but God can provide a lamp.

We can choose to walk by the light and lamp of God's Word, or we can choose to walk by our own sparks, by our own wisdom. The latter produces sorrow; the former produces rejoicing.

––––––––––––––––––

Isaiah 50:11
Behold, all ye that kindle a fire, that compass yourselves about with sparks: walk in the light of your fire, and in the sparks that ye have kindled. This shall ye have of mine hand; ye shall lie down in sorrow.

Psalm 119:105
Thy word is a lamp unto my feet, and a light unto my path.

Jeremiah 2:13
For my people have committed two evils; they have forsaken me the fountain of living waters, and hewed them out cisterns, broken cisterns, that can hold no water.

Chapter 5

Renewed Like the Eagle

Who satisfieth thy mouth with good things;
so that thy youth is renewed like the eagle's. Psalm 103:5

In the verse above, God promises to satisfy with good things so that one's youth is renewed like the eagle is renewed. To understand this verse, let's first consider the eagle.

It is noteworthy that eagles are mentioned and used as a comparison numerous times in the Bible. The eagle, like other comparisons, is mentioned in places where its characteristics help make a point. For instance, Deuteronomy 32 refers to God as an eagle fluttering over the young, spreading out His wings, and then bearing them on His wings.

Understanding some characteristics of eagles helps us to understand the comparisons. A mother eagle will stir up the nest, let the babies drop, and then catch them with her wings. This is how she teaches them to fly. Similarly, God wants His people to fly. He is so willing to catch us, help us, and carry us until we can indeed fly.

In Exodus 19:4, God reminds Moses that He bore the nation of Israel on eagles' wings. In other words, He carried the whole nation on His wings, just as a mother eagle would carry her young on her wings. That is quite a picture of God's great power, care, and concern.

Psalm 103 talks about youth being renewed as an eagle is renewed. How is the youth of an eagle renewed?

I have read various methods of how different types of eagles have to shed their old feathers. One method is that of the eagle plucking out every feather on his body until he is completely bare. He then stays in a hiding place until he grows new feathers.

Another method is when an eagle will shed his old cumbersome feathers by plunging into a body of water. At that point, the old feathers are shed. The eagle then stays close to shore protecting himself and eating what food he can while waiting for new feathers. Once he has his new feathers, his strength is renewed.

The book of Isaiah says that those who wait upon the Lord will "renew their strength; they shall mount up with wings as eagles; they shall run, and not be weary; and they shall walk, and not faint."

Our youth, or more literally, our spiritual walk with God, is renewed as we shed the old and get the new. There are a number of verses in the New Testament that refer to "putting off" and "putting on." We are to put off the old man and put on the new man.

Just like the eagle cannot get his new feathers until he gets rid of his old feathers, we too must put off, cast down, or lay aside the old, and then put on the new. We determine mentally that those old things will no longer be a part of our lives, and we replace them with what the Bible declares to be our new nature.

As we shed the old feathers and put on the new in their place, we are renewed. We can walk with Him and not faint. We can run with Him and not be weary. We can be renewed and mount up with wings of eagles.

Psalm 103:5
Who satisfieth thy mouth with good things; so that thy youth is renewed like the eagle's.

Deuteronomy 32:9-12
For the Lord's portion is his people; Jacob is the lot of his inheritance.

He found him in a desert land, and in the waste howling wilderness; he led him about, he instructed him, he kept him as the apple of his eye.

As an eagle stirreth up her nest, fluttereth over her young, spreadeth abroad her wings, taketh them, beareth them on her wings:

So the Lord alone did lead him, and there was no strange god with him.

Exodus 19:4
Ye have seen what I did unto the Egyptians, and how I bare you on eagles' wings, and brought you unto myself.

Isaiah 40:31
But they that wait upon the LORD shall renew their strength; they shall mount up with wings as eagles; they shall run, and not be weary; and they shall walk, and not faint.

Ephesians 4:22- 24
That ye put off concerning the former conversation the old man, which is corrupt according to the deceitful lusts;

And be renewed in the spirit of your mind;

And that ye put on the new man, which after God is created in righteousness and true holiness.

II Corinthians 10:5
Casting down imaginations, and every high thing that exalteth itself against the knowledge of God, and bringing into captivity every thought to the obedience of Christ;

Hebrews 12:1
Wherefore seeing we also are compassed about with so great a cloud of witnesses, let us lay aside every weight, and the sin which doth so easily beset us, and let us run with patience the race that is set before us.

Chapter 6

The Covenant of Salt

Ought ye not to know that the LORD God of Israel gave the kingdom over Israel to David forever, even to him and to his sons by a covenant of salt? II Chronicles 13:5

A covenant is an agreement or a contract. Today it is very common for people to enter into agreements by signing what we refer to as a contract. Not so long ago, they did it with a simple hand shake. One of the oldest known covenants in the world is the covenant of salt.

Salt is a necessity of life. Since ancient times it has been used in many cultures as a seasoning, a preservative, a disinfectant, a symbolic part of ceremonial offerings, and as a unit of exchange. The Bible contains numerous references to salt. In various contexts, it is used metaphorically to signify permanence, loyalty, durability, fidelity, usefulness, value, and purification.

The covenant of salt symbolizes loyalty and honesty. It represents that which is a lasting or preserved agreement. Some of the eastern people still use the phrase, "There is salt between us." In biblical times, they understood the covenant of salt meant they would keep their word at all costs. It was equivalent to a most solemn covenant.[7]

The most common way of entering a salt covenant was by eating food containing salt. The custom of pledging friendship or confirming an agreement or covenant by eating food containing salt is still retained today among some Middle Easterners. In fact, the Arabic word for salt and for an agreement or treaty is the same word.[8]

---

7   Janes M. Freeman, *Manners and Customs of the Bible* (reprinted 1972 by Logos International from original printing of Nelson and Phillips New York), 86
8   James A. Patch, "Salt" retrieved from https://www.internationalstandardbible.com/S/salt.html

Entering a covenant of salt was never done lightly or haphazardly. In biblical times, guests would eat their meals while their host stood. If the host did eat with his guests, that constituted as entering into a covenant of salt with them because the food contained salt.

Another noteworthy use of salt was when parents would rub their newborn babies with salt, symbolizing that they would grow up and keep their word.

In the late 1970's when Prime Minister Begin of Israel met with President Sadat of Egypt, Prime Minister Begin was greeted as he set foot on Egyptian soil. It was reported that the two men stopped to take bread and salt together.

To the western mind, this may seem like an old-fashioned custom, and one might think it was simply a nice gesture or photo opportunity but it was much more. In their eastern understanding, they entered into a salt covenant. Sadat was communicating through his actions that Begin would be safe while visiting Egypt, and he was willing to guarantee that safety with his own life.

Since ancient times in the Middle East, hospitality has been looked upon as an act of service to God. If one was traveling and needed shelter for the night, he could ask one of the Bedouin (a nomad of the region) for his protection and help by asking to partake of salt together. The Bedouin would then collect all his money and valuables, feed him, and give him a place to sleep. Finally, he would stand guard all night to make sure no harm came to the traveler.

In the morning, the Bedouin would feed him once again, return his valuables, and make sure he was safely on his way. Any kind of payment for his hospitality would never even be considered.

Perhaps you have attended weddings where salt was involved in the service. In many of the weddings I have officiated, couples who understood the significance of the covenant of salt requested to share salt during the ceremony. It symbolized the marriage being a lifelong, enduring covenant.

Having insight into this ancient covenant brings greater understanding when one reads the Scriptures. Jesus said, "You are the salt of the earth." And Paul exhorted, "Let your speech be always with grace, seasoned with salt."

Below are some verses making reference to the significance of salt and the covenant of salt.

II Chronicles 13:5
Ought ye not to know that the LORD God of Israel gave the kingdom over Israel to David for ever, even to him and to his sons by a covenant of salt?

Leviticus 2:13
And every oblation of thy meat offering shalt thou season with salt; neither shalt thou suffer the salt of the covenant of thy God to be lacking from thy meat offering: with all thine offerings thou shall offer salt.

Ezekiel 43:24
And thou shall offer them before the LORD, and the priests shall cast salt upon them, and they shall offer them up for a burnt offering unto the LORD.

Ezra 6:9
And that which they have need of, both young bullocks, and rams, and lambs, for the burnt offerings of the God of heaven, wheat, salt, wine, and oil, according to the appointment of the priests which are at Jerusalem, let it be given them day by day without fail:

Numbers 18:19
All the heave offerings of the holy things, which the children of Israel offer unto the LORD, have I given thee, and thy sons and thy daughters with thee, by a statute for ever: it is a covenant of salt for ever before the LORD unto thee and to thy seed with thee.

Matthew 5:13
Ye are the salt of the earth: but if the salt have lost his savour, wherewith shall it be salted? it is thenceforth good for nothing, but to be cast out, and to be trodden under foot of men.

Mark 9:50b
Have salt in yourselves, and have peace one with another.

Colossians 4:6
Let your speech be alway with grace, seasoned with salt, that ye may know how ye ought to answer every man.

Chapter 7

Swaddling Clothes

And she brought forth her firstborn son, and wrapped him in swaddling clothes, and laid him in a manger; because there was no room for them in the inn. Luke 2:7

Each December, many Christians all over the world remember the birth of Jesus Christ. The story has been retold through nativity scenes, plays, sermons, and other remembrances. One commonly misunderstood element is the swaddling clothes.

Most people understand they "laid him in a manger; because there was no room for them in the inn." If this is a familiar account, then it is understood that Bethlehem was rather crowded that evening, and all the inns were full.

A discussion of exactly what the manger may have looked like and where it was located is not the focus of this chapter. It is very significant to note, however, the savior of the world, the most important human being ever born, had some very humble beginnings. The King of Kings was laid in a manger.

There are some who assume because he was laid in a lowly manger instead of a big fancy hotel fit for a king that the swaddling clothes must have been some type of rags, or at best, some cheap clothes to keep him warm. Once again, an understanding of the eastern culture and customs brings great insight to this great event.

Bishop Pillai wrote, "The sons of kings and princes in the East today are still 'salted and swaddled.' A tiny bit of salt is rubbed on the baby to indicate that the parents intend to teach the child to be truthful. The baby is then wrapped in swaddling clothes. These are fine linen strips about two inches wide which are wrapped round and round the baby's body to straighten him out: arms and legs and all are made straight as a ramrod. This is a sign to God that the parents will rear the child to be straightforward before the Lord, and free from crookedness.

The child is left in this position from fifteen minutes to two hours, while the parents meditate and make their vows to God concerning their sacred trust which was given them when they received the child."[9] (The salting of a newborn Bishop mentions is in reference to the salt covenant. See Chapter 6)

While the biblical account of the birth of Jesus only mentions the swaddling clothes, it is understood to the eastern mind that he was both salted and swaddled. In the east, a child born to nobility or royalty would always be salted and swaddled, never just one of the two.

To say a person, especially of nobility, was not salted and swaddled was to say that they were dishonest, crooked, and had no integrity. Ezekiel 16:4 mentions not being salted and swaddled.

Swaddling clothes were only left on the baby for a short amount of time while the parents prayed and offered their vows to God. At the end of that time the swaddling clothes were removed, and the normal baby attire would be put on the child.

The angel told the shepherds that Christ had been born in Bethlehem and that they would find the babe lying in a manger, wrapped in swaddling clothes. One can certainly understand now why the Bible says the shepherds went in haste to Bethlehem to see the savior. They knew they needed to get there quickly if they were to see the savior of the world.

Isn't it amazing God sent an angel to announce the birth of His Son to some humble shepherds? God chose to reveal this wonderful occasion not to people of great stature and importance, not to the high priest in Jerusalem, and not to any religious or political leaders. What joy the shepherds must have had as they beheld the savior of the world, wrapped in swaddling clothes, lying in a manger.

What a night for them! What a night for the world!

9   Bishop K.C. Pillai, *Light Through an Eastern Window* (Robert Speller & Sons, New York, 1963),42

Luke 2:7-18

And she brought forth her firstborn son, and wrapped him in swaddling clothes, and laid him in a manger; because there was no room for them in the inn.

And there were in the same country shepherds abiding in the field, keeping watch over their flock by night.

And, lo, the angel of the Lord came upon them, and the glory of the Lord shone round about them: and they were sore afraid.

And the angel said unto them, Fear not: for, behold, I bring you good tidings of great joy, which shall be to all people. For unto you is born this day in the city of David a Saviour, which is Christ the Lord.

And this shall be a sign unto you; Ye shall find the babe wrapped in swaddling clothes, lying in a manger.

And suddenly there was with the angel a multitude of the heavenly host praising God, and saying,

Glory to God in the highest, and on earth peace, good will toward men.

And it came to pass, as the angels were gone away from them into heaven, the shepherds said one to another, Let us now go even unto Bethlehem, and see this thing which is come to pass, which the Lord hath made known unto us.

And they came with haste, and found Mary, and Joseph, and the babe lying in a manger.

And when they had seen it, they made known abroad the saying which was told them concerning this child.

And all they that heard it wondered at those things which were told them by the shepherds.

Ezekiel 16:4:
And as for thy nativity, in the day thou wast born thy navel was not cut, neither wast thou washed in water to supple thee; thou wast not salted at all, nor swaddled at all.

Chapter 8

Buy Wine and Milk Without Money

*Ho, every one that thirsteth, come ye to the waters, and he that hath
no money; come ye, buy, and eat; yea, come, buy wine and milk
without money and without price. Isaiah 55:1*

Growing up I can remember on a number occasions my dad saying,
"No one gives you something for nothing." He understood that even
if someone gave you something, someone paid for it somewhere along
the line.

In the verse above, it talks about buying without money. Understanding
the eastern culture gives great insight not only to the verse itself, but
also what the verse implies. It pertains to merchants in the marketplace
who sell goods. They would call out prices and shoppers would stop
and pay for the things they wished to purchase.

There are still several places like that today in some parts of the world.
A few years ago, my wife, Kathy, and I experienced The Grand Bazaar
in Istanbul, which is one of the largest and oldest covered markets in
the world with over 1,200 shops. I promise they are not shy about
calling out.

In biblical times, there were occasions when the merchant changed
from calling, "Come ye, buy and drink," to, "Come, buy water, wine
or milk without money and without price". This indicated a person was
celebrating a special occasion and the merchant was distributing gifts.
The refreshment had no cost because someone already paid the price
for it.[10]

When people heard a merchant crying that they knew it meant someone
was grateful to God for reaching a milestone in their life. Since one
cannot give gifts to God, bestowing kindness or gifts to others was

---

10   Bishop K.C. Pillai, "Isaiah" retrieved from http://www.biblecustoms.org/bishop-
kc-pillai/old-and-new-testament-orientalism/isaiah

considered giving a gift to God. One could go to a merchant and purchase all their water, wine, or milk and then the merchant, in turn, would give the product to others for free.

It is really the opposite of our western culture. Today, when someone reaches a milestone such as an anniversary or a birthday they expect to receive gifts in honor of the event. However, the eastern culture of the Bible was much different. They celebrated by doing something good for others.

Those hearing the merchant crying out, especially those who were in need could go and "buy without money." It was free to them because the price had already been paid. The benefactor would stay at the merchant's stand as people came to "buy without money," so they could then express their thanks to the one who paid the price.

In the days of Isaiah, everyone understood "buying without money." Students of the Bible also readily recognize a deeper truth, especially since Isaiah prophesied much about the coming redeemer. Mankind could never pay the price necessary for redemption, but God so loved the world that He gave His Son as payment for all of mankind. The price was paid in full.

Because of the completed work of Jesus Christ, we have redemption and salvation at no cost to us. That is why the Bible says we are saved by grace. Eternal life is a free gift to us.

My dad was right; someone always pays the price. Just as those who bought milk without money would express thanks to the benefactor who paid the price for them, we too can express our thanks to God, who paid the price for us.

Isaiah 55:1:
Ho, every one that thirsteth, come ye to the waters, and he that hath no money; come ye, buy, and eat; yea, come, buy wine and milk without money and without price.

John 3:16
For God so loved the world, that he gave his only begotten Son, that whosoever believeth in him should not perish, but have everlasting life.

Ephesians 2:8
For by grace are ye saved through faith; and that not of yourselves: it is the gift of God:

Romans 6:23
For the wages of sin is death; but the gift of God is eternal life through Jesus Christ our Lord.

Chapter 9

Weaning a Child

And when she had weaned him, she took him up with her,
with three bullocks, and one ephah of flour, and a bottle of wine,
and brought him unto the house of the LORD in Shiloh:
and the child was young. I Samuel 1:24

In the book of I Samuel, we read about a lady who was barren; her name was Hannah. In her culture, having a child was considered a blessing from God. Giving birth to a boy was the greatest blessing as they continued to look for and expect the Messiah. Not bearing a child was not only heartbreaking to a woman, but many also thought of it as a disgrace, an indication of a lack of blessing from God.

Hannah prayed. She promised God if He would bless her with a boy that she would give the child to the temple for God's service. That meant the child would grow up and spend his life in the temple in service to God.

God did indeed bless Hannah with a boy whose name was Samuel. She honored her vow and brought him to the temple after he was weaned. God multiplied His blessings in answering the prayer of Hannah by giving her five more children in addition to Samuel.

In reading the record, we learn Hannah brought Samuel to the temple after he was weaned. There has been discussion and debate as to how old Samuel was when Hannah brought him to the temple. E.W. Bullinger states Samuel could have been twelve years old when he was brought to the temple.[11]

According to Bishop Pillai, "Children in the East are weaned usually at about five years old. Two meanings of weaning. 1. When child finishes drinking the mother's milk; and 2. When the child has been taught the

---

11   E.W. Bullinger, *The Companion Bible* (Enlarged type edition, Kregal Publications, Grand Rapids Michigan, 1999), 368

milk of the Word. Both must be accomplished. The child sleeps with the mother and she teaches him to praise God. The child is presented to God at the temple after the child is weaned. It is the mother's responsibility to teach the Word to the children. Young Samuel was able to understand God, i.e., he was old enough to go to Eli in the night—he wasn't a baby."[12] Isn't that beautiful? The mother feeds her child both physical food and spiritual food.

The Scriptures in I Samuel state that when they brought Samuel to the temple he was a young child. They certainly wouldn't bring a six or eight-month-old to the temple. Samuel, a little boy, was brought to the temple for a lifetime of service. In his early years he lived and learned from Eli, the high priest and judge of Israel. Later, this young boy grew and walked with God, and he became one of the greatest prophets of all time.

I Samuel 1

Now there was a certain man of Ramathaimzophim, of mount Ephraim, and his name was Elkanah, the son of Jeroham, the son of Elihu, the son of Tohu, the son of Zuph, an Ephrathite:

And he had two wives; the name of the one was Hannah, and the name of the other Peninnah: and Peninnah had children, but Hannah had no children.

And this man went up out of his city yearly to worship and to sacrifice unto the LORD of hosts in Shiloh. And the two sons of Eli, Hophni and Phinehas, the priests of the LORD, were there.

And when the time was that Elkanah offered, he gave to Peninnah his wife, and to all her sons and her daughters, portions:

But unto Hannah he gave a worthy portion; for he loved Hannah: but the LORD had shut up her womb.

And her adversary also provoked her sore, for to make her fret, because the LORD had shut up her womb.

12   Bishop K.C. Pillai, "I Samuel" retrieved from http://www.biblecustoms.org/bishop-kc-pillai/old-and-new-testament-orientalism/i-samuel

And as he did so year by year, when she went up to the house of the LORD, so she provoked her; therefore she wept, and did not eat.

Then said Elkanah her husband to her, Hannah, why weepest thou? and why eatest thou not? and why is thy heart grieved? am not I better to thee than ten sons?

So Hannah rose up after they had eaten in Shiloh, and after they had drunk. Now Eli the priest sat upon a seat by a post of the temple of the LORD.

And she was in bitterness of soul, and prayed unto the LORD, and wept sore.

And she vowed a vow, and said, O LORD of hosts, if thou wilt indeed look on the affliction of thine handmaid, and remember me, and not forget thine handmaid, but wilt give unto thine handmaid a man child, then I will give him unto the LORD all the days of his life, and there shall no razor come upon his head.

And it came to pass, as she continued praying before the LORD, that Eli marked her mouth.

Now Hannah, she spake in her heart; only her lips moved, but her voice was not heard: therefore Eli thought she had been drunken.

And Eli said unto her, How long wilt thou be drunken? put away thy wine from thee.

And Hannah answered and said, No, my lord, I am a woman of a sorrowful spirit: I have drunk neither wine nor strong drink, but have poured out my soul before the LORD.

Count not thine handmaid for a daughter of Belial: for out of the abundance of my complaint and grief have I spoken hitherto.

Then Eli answered and said, Go in peace: and the God of Israel grant thee thy petition that thou hast asked of him.

And she said, Let thine handmaid find grace in thy sight. So the woman went her way, and did eat, and her countenance was no more sad.

And they rose up in the morning early, and worshipped before the LORD, and returned, and came to their house to Ramah: and Elkanah knew Hannah his wife; and the LORD remembered her.

Wherefore it came to pass, when the time was come about after Hannah had conceived, that she bare a son, and called his name Samuel, saying, Because I have asked him of the LORD.

And the man Elkanah, and all his house, went up to offer unto the LORD the yearly sacrifice, and his vow.

But Hannah went not up; for she said unto her husband, I will not go up until the child be weaned, and then I will bring him, that he may appear before the LORD, and there abide for ever.

And Elkanah her husband said unto her, Do what seemeth thee good; tarry until thou have weaned him; only the LORD establish his word. So the woman abode, and gave her son suck until she weaned him.

And when she had weaned him, she took him up with her, with three bullocks, and one ephah of flour, and a bottle of wine, and brought him unto the house of the LORD in Shiloh: and the child was young.

And they slew a bullock, and brought the child to Eli.

And she said, Oh my lord, as thy soul liveth, my lord, I am the woman that stood by thee here, praying unto the LORD.

For this child I prayed; and the LORD hath given me my petition which I asked of him:

Therefore also I have lent him to the LORD; as long as he liveth he shall be lent to the LORD. And he worshipped the LORD there.

I Samuel 2:2 and 21
And Eli blessed Elkanah and his wife, and said, The LORD give thee seed of this woman for the loan which is lent to the LORD. And they went unto their own home.

And the LORD visited Hannah, so that she conceived, and bare three sons and two daughters. And the child Samuel grew before the LORD.

I Peter 2:2
As newborn babes, desire the sincere milk of the word, that ye may grow thereby:

I Corinthians 2:2
I have fed you with milk, and not with meat: for hitherto ye were not able to bear it, neither yet now are ye able.

Chapter 10

Bewailed Her Virginity

And he said, Go. And he sent her away for two months: and she went with her companions, and bewailed her virginity upon the mountains.
Judges 11:38

This chapter addresses a misunderstanding of a burnt offering and gives some insight on bewailing virginity and rending clothes. Understanding the biblical culture sheds light on this record about Jephthah making a vow unto the Lord.

The Ammonites and Israelites were at war. Before Jephthah went to battle, he made a vow to God. Jephthah told God if he won the battle that when he came back victorious, the first person to come to him would be given to the Lord as a burnt offering.

God granted Jephthah the victory. When he returned home, he was greeted by his only child, his daughter, who came rejoicing to meet her dad unaware of his vow. When Jephthah saw her, he immediately rent his clothes.

The eastern people dress with underclothing, often referred to as a tunic, and then with a long piece of clothing that hangs from the shoulders to the ankles called a robe or cloak. Over this they wear a garment that hangs from the shoulders to the knees only; this is called a coat. Finally, they wear or hang a mantle.

A mantle is usually a piece of white cloth three or four yards long and 18 to 20 inches wide. They fold it over and over until it is four to six inches wide yet still the same length. They wear it folded about the neck and let it hang down to the knees or even below. When this cloth or garment is folded the Bible refers to it as a mantle.

The mantle is a sign of authority and power. The expression, "rent his clothes," means to tear one's mantle. It doesn't mean they ripped or tore all their clothing. They ripped or tore their mantle as an outward sign of either anger or sorrow. The eastern people did this to indicate to those around them what was going on inside of their hearts.

Jephthah, because it was his only daughter and only child who first met him, rent his mantle. He then told his daughter that he had opened his mouth unto God and could not go back on what he told God. He was a man of integrity.

Jephthah had vowed to offer his daughter as a burnt offering to God, but the term burnt offering has two meanings. One meaning of burnt offering is to sacrifice an animal. The other meaning is to give oneself to serve in the temple, which is what is meant in the record we are considering.[13]

It is referred to as a burnt offering because a young woman given to service in the temple suffers. She could never marry, which was disgraceful and humiliating in their culture. That was part of the shame she suffered.

She also could not have children. This was also very humiliating to a woman in that culture. Those who chose to give their lives in service to the temple endured that shame. Thus, it was referred to as a burnt offering.

Jephthah's daughter understood the situation, and she asked her father if she could first go and "bewail her virginity." In that culture, a woman who wanted to give herself in service to God had to be a virgin. The expression, "bewail her virginity," means that she would spend two months in preparation before joining herself to the temple. She would go with her close friends to see relatives and other acquaintances and say her goodbyes.

She would also spend time with those close companions in prayer, sanctifying and consecrating herself in preparation for leaving that life behind and coming to the temple to give her life in service to God. She would do this for two months.

---

13   Bishop K.C. Pillai, *Light Through an Eastern Window* (Robert Speller & Sons, New York, 1963), 118

"Bewailing of virginity" simply means preparing to be a servant in the temple. After two months her father would take her to the temple; her head was shaved, and she put a veil on her head. She then worked and lived in the temple. She never left.

This record in Judges ends by saying that the daughters of Israel went yearly to lament the daughter of Jephthah. Because of the English word "lament" and a misunderstanding of the two types of burnt offerings, some have erroneously concluded Jephthah's daughter being sacrificed meant that she was brought to the temple and killed.

The Hebrew word translated "lament" in the King James Version would be much more accurately translated "talk with." She certainly was not dead; her friends even came to see her for a few days every year. They would have praised her for all she was doing in keeping her father's promise to God. They would have praised her for agreeing to suffer the shame of not being married or having children. It must have been a very special time of the year for her.

In that culture the children were trained to follow what their father said. To them, their father's word was God's word. That was the culture. That is why she told her father, Jephthah, that whatever he told God, she would do.

The most striking and inspiring thing to me in this record is that Jephthah said he could not go back on his word, on the promise he made to God. In that culture, what one said one must do, at all costs. What a man of integrity, indeed.

He did not go to God and ask for a compromise. He did not try to explain to God she was his only daughter and what all the ramifications would be, not only to her but to his life also as the judge for Israel at that time. There are a lot of things he could have said to God, but instead, he kept his word: "I cannot go back!"

Again, with a little understanding of the times and culture in which the Scriptures were written, the Bible becomes clear, and its richness shines brightly.

Judges 11:30 - 40

And Jephthah vowed a vow unto the LORD, and said, If thou shalt without fail deliver the children of Ammon into mine hands,

Then it shall be, that whatsoever cometh forth of the doors of my house to meet me, when I return in peace from the children of Ammon, shall surely be the LORD'S, and I will offer it up for a burnt offering.

So Jephthah passed over unto the children of Ammon to fight against them; and the LORD delivered them into his hands.

And he smote them from Aroer, even till thou come to Minnith, even twenty cities, and unto the plain of the vineyards, with a very great slaughter. Thus the children of Ammon were subdued before the children of Israel.

And Jephthah came to Mizpeh unto his house, and, behold, his daughter came out to meet him with timbrels and with dances: and she was his only child; beside her he had neither son nor daughter.

And it came to pass, when he saw her, that he rent his clothes, and said, Alas, my daughter! thou hast brought me very low, and thou art one of them that trouble me: for I have opened my mouth unto the LORD, and I cannot go back.

And she said unto him, My father, if thou hast opened thy mouth unto the LORD, do to me according to that which hath proceeded out of thy mouth; forasmuch as the LORD hath taken vengeance for thee of thine enemies, even of the children of Ammon.

And she said unto her father, Let this thing be done for me: let me alone two months, that I may go up and down upon the mountains, and bewail my virginity, I and my fellows.

And he said, Go. And he sent her away for two months: and she went with her companions, and bewailed her virginity upon the mountains.

And it came to pass at the end of two months, that she returned unto her father, who did with her according to his vow which he had vowed: and she knew no man. And it was a custom in Israel,

That the daughters of Israel went yearly to lament [talk with] the daughter of Jephthah the Gileadite four days in a year.

Chapter 11

An Ass's Head and Dove's Dung

*And there was a great famine in Samaria: and, behold, they besieged
it, until an ass's head was sold for fourscore pieces of silver,
and the fourth part of a cab of dove's dung for five pieces of silver.*
II Kings 6:25

One of the main reasons people do not believe the Bible is because they
do not understand it. How can one believe and trust the Bible as the
Word of God if one does not understand what he or she is reading?

A good example of this is in II Kings where it talks about a famine
in Samaria that was so horrible people were selling "ass's heads" and
"dove's dung" for food. Without understanding the eastern culture that
sounds ridiculous. However, it sounds no more ridiculous than it would
to someone unfamiliar with western culture who heard people in the
United States eat buffalo wings.

In the lands, times, and culture of the Bible, an "ass's head" was what
they called a root that grew in the hedges. It was not very tasty; in fact,
only cows or donkeys would eat it.

"Dove's dung" was a kind of a pea, like a chickpea, also not very tasty,
which was fed to doves. During the time of this famine in Samaria, the
Bible says that a fourth part of a cab of dove's dung was sold for five
pieces of silver. A cab was a dry measure holding nearly two quarts.[14]

Likewise, during this famine, an ass's head sold for around 80 pieces
of silver. That's a lot of money for a little root. This great famine was
caused by the besieging of the enemy. This kind of military strategy
sealed off a city to keep anyone from going in or out. The invading
army then waited until those in the city either surrendered or starved
to death.

14   Janes M. Freeman, *Manners and Customs of the Bible* (reprinted 1972 by Logos
International from original printing of Nelson and Phillips New York), 174

During this famine inside the city of Samaria, "ass's heads" and "dove's dung" were selling for some outrageous prices, but if someone was starving and had the money, price didn't matter.

In the record found in Chapters 6 and 7 of II Kings, one will discover something truly remarkable. Within a 24-hour period, there was a drastic change in that city's economy. The change was so great that a measure (about a peck, or a quarter of a bushel) of fine flour was then selling for one shekel, and about a half a bushel of barley was also selling for one shekel.

God not only shows the severity of that famine, but He also shows the great deliverance He brought to His people. There is no situation too difficult for God. Reading an account like the famine in Samaria gives us confidence in God to help us in our own circumstances, regardless of how desperate or severe they appear to us.

II Kings 6:25
And there was a great famine in Samaria: and, behold, they besieged it, until an ass's head was sold for fourscore pieces of silver, and the fourth part of a cab of dove's dung for five pieces of silver.

II Kings 7:1 and 18
Then Elisha said, Hear ye the word of the LORD; Thus saith the LORD, Tomorrow about this time shall a measure of fine flour be sold for a shekel, and two measures of barley for a shekel, in the gate of Samaria.

And it came to pass as the man of God had spoken to the king, saying, Two measures of barley for a shekel, and a measure of fine flour for a shekel, shall be tomorrow about this time in the gate of Samaria.

(Note: The entire account of this famine and the subsequent deliverance is found in II Kings 6:24-7:19)

Chapter 12

I Am Pharaoh

*And Pharaoh said unto Joseph, I am Pharaoh, and without thee
shall no man lift up his hand or foot in all the land of Egypt.*
Genesis 41:44

The remarkable account of Joseph can be found in Genesis 37-50. If
this is a familiar account, one will recall Pharaoh called for Joseph, who
was in prison, to interpret Pharaoh's dream.

However, as one reads what is recorded after Joseph interpreted
Pharaoh's dream, the above verse seems a bit odd. Pharaoh said to
Joseph, "I am Pharaoh, and without you shall no man lift up his hand
or foot in all the land of Egypt." Why did Pharaoh tell him, "I am
Pharaoh"?

At this point in the record, Pharaoh was giving Joseph authority over
all of Egypt. He was, in fact, placing Joseph as second only to himself.
This was an extraordinary event that only Pharaoh could command.

Saying, "I am," was a declaration that what he was speaking was as
good as who he was. When someone says, "I am so-and-so," they
are attesting that what they are saying is absolutely certain. It is a
declaration of one's prestige, standing, status, power, and authority.

Obviously, Joseph knew who he was standing before. Pharaoh gave
what we might refer to as an executive order. He was making it very
clear there could be no question as to the certainty of what he spoke.

This expression is very similar to when someone says, "In the name
of..." In that case, it is not the person himself speaking, but someone
else on his behalf who has the authority to speak using his name. Again,
it would mean all the authority, power, status, standing, and prestige of
that name.

In our culture in the United States, it would be a bit awkward in the workplace to say, "In the name of the boss, this project is a priority." We would simply say, "The boss said to get this done."

For Christians today, as born-again believers, we have the authority to utilize the name of Jesus Christ.

In the book of Acts, there are a number of references to believers operating the power of God utilizing the name of Jesus Christ. We can, and should, pray in the name of Jesus Christ. We can, and should, operate the power of God in the name of Jesus Christ.

Genesis 41:44
And Pharaoh said unto Joseph, I am Pharaoh, and without thee shall no man lift up his hand or foot in all the land of Egypt.

[For the complete record concerning Joseph, see Genesis 37 – 50]

Acts 3:6, 16
Then Peter said, Silver and gold have I none; but such as I have give I thee: In the name of Jesus Christ of Nazareth rise up and walk.

And his name through faith in his name hath made this man strong, whom ye see and know: yea, the faith which is by him hath given him this perfect soundness in the presence of you all.

Acts 4:10
Be it known unto you all, and to all the people of Israel, that by the name of Jesus Christ of Nazareth, whom ye crucified, whom God raised from the dead, even by him doth this man stand here before you whole.

Acts 9:34
And Peter said unto him, Aeneas, Jesus Christ maketh thee whole: arise, and make thy bed. And he arose immediately.

Acts 8:12
But when they believed Philip preaching the things concerning the kingdom of God, and the name of Jesus Christ, they were baptized, both men and women.

Acts 16:18
And this did she many days. But Paul, being grieved, turned and said to the spirit, I command thee in the name of Jesus Christ to come out of her. And he came out the same hour.

Ephesians 5:20
Giving thanks always for all things unto God and the Father in the name of our Lord Jesus Christ;

Mark 9:39
But Jesus said, Forbid him not: for there is no man which shall do a miracle in my name, that can lightly speak evil of me.

John 14:13 and 14
And whatsoever ye shall ask in my name, that will I do, that the Father may be glorified in the Son.

If ye shall ask any thing in my name, I will do *it*.

John 20:31
But these are written, that ye might believe that Jesus is the Christ, the Son of God; and that believing ye might have life through his name.

Chapter 13

Leaving Egypt with Silver, Gold, and Raiment

And the children of Israel did according to the word of Moses; and they borrowed of the Egyptians jewels of silver, and jewels of gold, and raiment:

And the LORD gave the people favour in the sight of the Egyptians, so that they lent unto them such things as they required. And they spoiled the Egyptians. Exodus 12:35, 36

According to the record in Exodus 12, the children of Israel did not leave Egypt empty-handed. Quite the contrary, they left with tremendous wealth. This is perhaps puzzling to the western mind, maybe even ludicrous. Why would the Egyptians give these people their silver, gold, and raiment?

In biblical times, it was very common to borrow jewels or raiment for a pilgrimage because a pilgrimage was understood to have God involved in it; it was seen as a spiritual matter. In that culture it was thought that if one helped someone else who was going on a pilgrimage, the lender was also taking part in the things of God.

In this record, the use of the words "borrow" and "lent" are very noteworthy. If one lent an item and never received it back, he did not worry about it because he knew he was giving to a godly or spiritual cause. That is why the words "borrow" and "lent" were used.

The children of Israel were leaving to go worship their God; that made it a pilgrimage. In Chapter 11, God instructed Moses to tell the children of Israel to borrow from the Egyptians for their pilgrimage. Given all the recent horrific events the people of Egypt had witnessed, they would have been more than glad to give to a spiritual pilgrimage.

Exodus 11:2
Speak now in the ears of the people, and let every man borrow of his neighbour, and every woman of her neighbour, jewels of silver, and jewels of gold.

Exodus 12:35 and 36
And the children of Israel did according to the word of Moses; and they borrowed of the Egyptians jewels of silver, and jewels of gold, and raiment:

And the LORD gave the people favour in the sight of the Egyptians, so that they lent unto them such things as they required. And they spoiled the Egyptians.

Psalm 105:36
He brought them forth also with silver and gold: and there was not one feeble person among their tribes.

Chapter 14

The Harlot Rahab

And Joshua the son of Nun sent out of Shittim two men to spy secretly, saying, Go view the land, even Jericho. And they went, and came into an harlot's house, named Rahab, and lodged there. Joshua 2:1

Many believe, and some are even adamant, that Rahab in the story of Joshua and Jericho was a prostitute. Some scholars point out that the Hebrew word used in the Old Testament as well as the Greek word used in the New Testament clearly indicate that fact. Was she really a prostitute, though?

The meaning of a word is very important, but one also needs to consider figures of speech and the culture in which the Bible was written. For example, Jesus Christ referred to Herod as a fox. While Herod may have had many attributes of a fox, he was still a man. Discerning the metaphor, we understand what Jesus was talking about when he called Herod a fox.

To better understand Rahab, we need to consider women, inns, and prostitutes in biblical times. Women covered their faces with veils. They did not talk to any men except their husbands and relatives. To be unveiled or to talk to strangers was a breach in culture for them.

Inns in biblical times were located either on the roadside or at the gate of a city, which was the case in the story of Rahab. These inns were publicly funded, and there was no charge for the travelers.

It was not common for a woman to be an innkeeper. The job would first be offered to men. If there were no men willing to take the job, it was then offered to women. A woman taking the job would not be veiled, which would be breaking her cultural norm.

She would be serving the public, meaning she would be unveiled talking to strange men. She had made the choice to get rid of her veil and serve anybody and everybody.

Prostitutes in that culture were not allowed to live in the city. They, along with swine herders, lepers, and alcohol shops, were kept a good distance from the city—in some cases as far as three miles away.

The Bible tells us that Rahab lived on the town wall at the gate of the city. This was where the inn would have been. We also learn from the Scriptures that Rahab's family lived with her, which was typical for innkeepers.

Because this unique situation was so contrary to their cultural norm, the word "harlot" became a title for women who were innkeepers. Rahab was an innkeeper, not a prostitute.[15]

There are some who object to saying Rahab was a prostitute only because they think that would make her a filthy sinner, and God would never employ her help. Others embrace the idea that she was a prostitute because they feel it shows God loves everyone.

Regardless of feelings or opinions, considering the culture in which the Bible was written helps us to see and rightly understand God's Word. It is also noteworthy that Rahab the harlot is listed in Hebrews 11 right there with some of the great believers of all time.

———————————

Joshua 2:1- 21
And Joshua the son of Nun sent out of Shittim two men to spy secretly, saying, Go view the land, even Jericho. And they went, and came into an harlot's house, named Rahab, and lodged there.

And it was told the king of Jericho, saying, Behold, there came men in hither to night of the children of Israel to search out the country.

And the king of Jericho sent unto Rahab, saying, Bring forth the men that are come to thee, which are entered into thine house: for they be come to search out all the country.

And the woman took the two men, and hid them, and said thus, There came men unto me, but I wist not whence they were:

15   Walter J. Cummins, *A Journey through the Acts and Epistles, Volume 2* (Scripture Consulting Franklin, Ohio, 2013), 60

And it came to pass about the time of shutting of the gate, when it was dark, that the men went out: whither the men went I wot not: pursue after them quickly; for ye shall overtake them.

But she had brought them up to the roof of the house, and hid them with the stalks of flax, which she had laid in order upon the roof.

And the men pursued after them the way to Jordan unto the fords: and as soon as they which pursued after them were gone out, they shut the gate.

And before they were laid down, she came up unto them upon the roof;

And she said unto the men, I know that the LORD hath given you the land, and that your terror is fallen upon us, and that all the inhabitants of the land faint because of you.

For we have heard how the LORD dried up the water of the Red sea for you, when ye came out of Egypt; and what ye did unto the two kings of the Amorites, that were on the other side Jordan, Sihon and Og, whom ye utterly destroyed.

And as soon as we had heard these things, our hearts did melt, neither did there remain any more courage in any man, because of you: for the LORD your God, he is God in heaven above, and in earth beneath.

Now therefore, I pray you, swear unto me by the LORD, since I have showed you kindness, that ye will also show kindness unto my father's house, and give me a true token:

And that ye will save alive my father, and my mother, and my brethren, and my sisters, and all that they have, and deliver our lives from death.

And the men answered her, Our life for yours, if ye utter not this our business. And it shall be, when the LORD hath given us the land, that we will deal kindly and truly with thee.

Then she let them down by a cord through the window: for her house was upon the town wall, and she dwelt upon the wall.

And she said unto them, Get you to the mountain, lest the pursuers meet you; and hide yourselves there three days, until the pursuers be returned: and afterward may ye go your way.

And the men said unto her, We will be blameless of this thine oath which thou hast made us swear.

Behold, when we come into the land, thou shalt bind this line of scarlet thread in the window which thou didst let us down by: and thou shalt bring thy father, and thy mother, and thy brethren, and all thy father's household, home unto thee.

And it shall be, that whosoever shall go out of the doors of thy house into the street, his blood shall be upon his head, and we will be guiltless: and whosoever shall be with thee in the house, his blood shall be on our head, if any hand be upon him.

And if thou utter this our business, then we will be quit of thine oath which thou hast made us to swear.

And she said, According unto your words, so be it. And she sent them away, and they departed: and she bound the scarlet line in the window.

Joshua 6:21-23
And they utterly destroyed all that was in the city, both man and woman, young and old, and ox, and sheep, and ass, with the edge of the sword.

But Joshua had said unto the two men that had spied out the country, Go into the harlot's house, and bring out thence the woman, and all that she hath, as ye sware unto her.

And the young men that were spies went in, and brought out Rahab, and her father, and her mother, and her brethren, and all that she had; and they brought out all her kindred, and left them without the camp of Israel.

Hebrews 11:31
By faith [believing] the harlot Rahab perished not with them that believed not, when she had received the spies with peace.

Chapter 15

In the Street

The stranger did not lodge in the street:
but I opened my doors to the traveler. Job 31:32

In our culture, thinking of someone spending the night in the street conjures up all sorts of unpleasant pictures. However, when reading the Bible, one must always remember the culture in which it was written.

The verse above talks about a stranger who "did not lodge in the street." Instead, someone opened his doors to the traveler. This was very common in the lands and times of the Bible.

In small villages, there was usually a common area similar to what we call a park. Here and other places in the Bible refer to it as "the street." In the late afternoon or early evening, it was very common for travelers to rest and spend the night in that area of the village.

In biblical times, hospitality was extremely important. People believed if they showed kindness to someone in need, they were showing kindness to God. They believed if they gave something to someone, even a cup of water, it was understood it had been given as unto God.

In that culture they believed the more they served others, the more they served God. That is why it was common for them to invite travelers, who would be total strangers to them, to spend the night in their homes instead of in the street. They invited them to their homes to show them hospitality; they opened their doors. Thist is what Lot did when the angels came to Sodom.

There is a verse in the book of Hebrews that talks about remembering to show kindness to strangers as there have been some who did so not knowing those strangers were actually angels. That is something to consider, isn't it?

Job 31:32
The stranger did not lodge in the street: *but* I opened my doors to the traveler.

Genesis 19:1-3
And there came two angels to Sodom at even; and Lot sat in the gate of Sodom: and Lot seeing them rose up to meet them; and he bowed himself with his face toward the ground;

And he said, Behold now, my lords, turn in, I pray you, into your servant's house, and tarry all night, and wash your feet, and ye shall rise up early, and go on your ways. And they said, Nay; but we will abide in the street all night.

And he pressed upon them greatly; and they turned in unto him, and entered into his house; and he made them a feast, and did bake unleavened bread, and they did eat.

Hebrews 13:2
Be not forgetful to entertain strangers: for thereby some have entertained angels unawares.

Chapter 16

The Partridge Sits on Eggs

As the partridge sits on eggs, and hatches them not; so he that gets riches, and not by right, shall leave them in the midst of his days, and at his end shall be a fool. Jeremiah 17:11

This verse in Jeremiah uses an example of a partridge to address obtaining riches the wrong way. It talks about the partridge sitting on her eggs but not hatching them. Understanding why the partridge would not hatch the eggs gives great insight about seeking riches the wrong way.

There are numerous verses in the Bible that talk about money. Money itself is not evil; it is the love of money that is the root of all evil. One can read about a number of wonderful believers in the Bible who were wealthy. However, obtaining riches the wrong way is addressed as well.

Partridges are birds in the pheasant family. They are a non-migratory group that are medium-sized birds, intermediate between the larger pheasants and the smaller quails. Partridges are native to Europe, Asia, Africa, and the Middle East. Partridges are ground-nesting seed-eaters.

The partridge lays eggs in a small hole in the sand, and then sits on them. However, they are very skittish, fearful birds. If they are startled, they will flee and abandon their eggs.

Those who seek to obtain riches by unethical means will lose those riches. Just as a partridge will leave her eggs and not return, so shall it be for those who get riches unethically.

The Bible says those who will be rich will fall into many temptations. There will be temptations that those who do not have riches will not be tempted with. While that is a great caution, it is certainly not an admonition to not be wealthy.

The Bible also talks about instructing those who are rich not to be egotistical and not to trust in their riches because those riches are always uncertain. Instead, just like everyone else, they should trust in the living God who richly gives us all things to enjoy.

If God thinks it is wrong to have wealth, His Word would have had different instructions for the wealthy. However, He instructs those believers who are rich to do good, be rich in good works, ready to distribute, and willing to share.

Some Christians believe money is evil and people who have wealth and prosperity need to give it all away to those less fortunate. The Bible teaches that giving of one's abundance is a choice each one of us makes, and it is not to be compulsory.

In his book, *Poverty Vs Wealth,* my friend, Roger Braker, wrote, "There are promises of prosperity to those that seek after God. That is an important principle to understand. As long as God comes first in your life, as long as you trust in Him, He (God) has many blessings, promises in store for you."[16]

Jeremiah 17:11
As the partridge sits on eggs, and hatches them not; so he that gets riches, and not by right, shall leave them in the midst of his days, and at his end shall be a fool.

I Timothy 6:9 and 10
But they that will be rich fall into temptation and a snare, and into many foolish and hurtful lusts, which drown men in destruction and perdition.

For the love of money is the root of all evil: which while some coveted after, they have erred from the faith, and pierced themselves through with many sorrows.

I Timothy 6:17 and 18
Charge them that are rich in this world, that they be not highminded,

16   Roger Braker, *Poverty vs Wealth* (Roger Braker, Oklahoma City, Oklahoma 2016), 27

nor trust in uncertain riches, but in the living God, who giveth us richly all things to enjoy;

That they do good, that they be rich in good works, ready to distribute, willing to communicate;

II Corinthians 9:6-8
But this I say, He which soweth sparingly shall reap also sparingly; and he which soweth bountifully shall reap also bountifully.

Every man according as he purposeth in his heart, so let him give; not grudgingly, or of necessity: for God loveth a cheerful giver.

And God is able to make all grace abound toward you; that ye, always having all sufficiency in all things, may abound to every good work:

Deuteronomy 8:18
But thou shalt remember the LORD thy God: for it is he that giveth thee power to get wealth, that he may establish his covenant which he sware unto thy fathers, as it is this day.

Chapter 17

Good Measure, Pressed Down, Shaken Together

Give, and it shall be given unto you; good measure, pressed down, and shaken together, and running over, shall men give into your bosom. For with the same measure that ye mete withal it shall be measured to you again. Luke 6:38

Like many other people, I practice the act of giving. Some call it the tithe, others refer to it as abundant sharing, and still others say it is the Law of Giving and Receiving. Understanding the marketplace in biblical times gives us great insight into something Jesus spoke about concerning the act of giving recorded in Luke 6.

Among Christians, there are many differences of opinion concerning the act of giving. Some teach that one must give ten percent or tithe of one's increase, while others say that we are no longer under the Old Testament Law and do not need to tithe. The case is then made that Abraham tithed long before the Old Testament Law, and the arguments and debates continue.

There are numerous discussions on this topic such as: Who should receive one's giving? Should one give of net or gross pay? How frequently should one give? The purpose of this chapter is not to answer any of those questions, but rather, to glean a tremendous truth that Jesus spoke concerning the act of giving.

In this record in Luke's Gospel, Jesus said, "Give, and it shall be given unto you; good measure, pressed down, and shaken together, and running over, shall men give into your bosom." He added that with the same measure one gives, it will be measured to him again.

At first glance, this "same measure" seems puzzling. Receiving back the same measure that one gave does not sound like "running over" does it? Plus, receiving back the "same measure" one gave does not sound like what Malachi states about giving and then God opening the windows of heaven to pour out His blessing.

I was sitting in a teaching many years ago where the teacher demonstrated this "pressed down, shaken together, and running over." I have, on occasion, demonstrated it to my audience. It is how they operated in the eastern marketplace.

Let's say a person brings a container to buy a certain amount or measure of barley. The merchant measures out that amount and puts it into the container. Then, the merchant does something quite remarkable.

He will press down that measure of barley in the container, shake it, press it down again, and then shake it again. As a result, the container is no longer full. It has been compressed.

The merchant then adds more barley and once again presses and shakes it down. He continues this process until he cannot get any more into the container, and it is literally running over the sides. That, in their mind, is a good measure.

So, while the price paid was for that one measure, what was received was much more than the one measure. Jesus was teaching as one gives, God will bless the giver back with more than what was given.

Some people do not understand the great Law of Giving and Receiving. There are those who think they have so little to begin with, they cannot give. Yet in not giving, they miss out on receiving back more than what they would have given.

Many years ago, I struggled with this idea of giving what I earned. I did not have very much to begin with and did not want to give some of it away. I did not understand the Law of Giving and Receiving. Then I learned two things that helped me tremendously.

First, I learned that everything belongs to God—everything! Oh, I may have put in the time and labor on the job, but where did my mind and body come from? Who gave me life in the first place? Everything originally came from the Creator, and the Bible says it all belongs to Him.

Second, I learned God set up the Law of Giving and Receiving so that both the giver and the receiver would be blessed. In other words, when one gives, one receives back. Since that time back in 1976, I have been a consistent giver, and God has consistently blessed me back.

It is also noteworthy to consider all of life has its cycles; there are ups and downs and highs and lows throughout all of creation. I have seen His blessings in my life in the abundant times and in the lean times. I have also seen very clearly over the years a person can never, ever out-give God.

This Law of Giving and Receiving is one of those universal laws that works for anyone. Just like gravity, one does not have to be a Christian to take advantage of operating this wonderful law. When Jesus taught that day, he painted a vivid picture to help the listeners understand.

Luke 6:38
Give, and it shall be given unto you; good measure, pressed down, and shaken together, and running over, shall men give into your bosom. For with the same measure that ye mete withal it shall be measured to you again.

II Corinthians 9:6-11
But this I say, He which soweth sparingly shall reap also sparingly; and he which soweth bountifully shall reap also bountifully.

Every man according as he purposeth in his heart, so let him give; not grudgingly, or of necessity: for God loveth a cheerful giver.

And God is able to make all grace abound toward you; that ye, always having all sufficiency in all things, may abound to every good work:

(As it is written, He hath dispersed abroad; he hath given to the poor: his righteousness remaineth for ever.

Now he that ministereth seed to the sower both minister bread for your food, and multiply your seed sown, and increase the fruits of your righteousness;)

Being enriched in every thing to all bountifulness, which causeth through us thanksgiving to God.

Malachi 3:10 and 11
Bring ye all the tithes into the storehouse, that there may be meat in mine house, and prove me now herewith, saith the LORD of hosts, if I

will not open you the windows of heaven, and pour you out a blessing, that there shall not be room enough to receive it.

And I will rebuke the devourer for your sakes, and he shall not destroy the fruits of your ground; neither shall your vine cast her fruit before the time in the field, saith the LORD of hosts.

Deuteronomy 10:14
Behold, the heaven and the heaven of heavens is the LORD'S thy God, the earth also, with all that therein is.

Chapter 18

Parables

Therefore speak I to them in parables: because they seeing see not; and hearing they hear not, neither do they understand. Matthew 13:13

I thought it might be helpful to offer a brief explanation of parables since Jesus often used parables when he taught, and some subsequent chapters in this book involve parables. Just like it is important to understand customs, idioms, and manners of biblical times, it is also important to understand parables.

A parable is a figure of speech. According to *New Thayer's Greek-English Lexicon*, a parable is "a comparing; a comparison of one thing with another." Similarly, Bullinger's *Critical Lexicon and Concordance to the English and Greek New Testament* states that the Greek word translated as parable is "a placing beside, or side by side, for the purpose of comparison."[17]

A parable is a fictitious story designed to teach a lesson through comparison. One benefit of a parable is it tells a story that is easy to remember. Many times, people and things in a parable represent things that are much more important than they seem to be on the surface, and the story imparts an important lesson.

It is sometimes shocking to people when they discover Jesus taught in parables to conceal the meaning of what he was sharing. In Chapter 13 of the Gospel of Matthew, Jesus explained why he taught the multitudes in parables when the disciples questioned him about it. He told them the people's hearts were waxed gross and their ears were dull of hearing. In other words, they did not really have a hunger to know. In contrast, the disciples wanted to learn so they asked Jesus to explain the parables.

---

17   E.W. Bullinger, *A Critical Lexicon and Concordance to the English and Greek New Testament* (Zondervan Printing 1975), 569

Bullinger also defines a parable as "enigmatic speech, a dark saying, opposite to plain speech; the teaching is not in the words, but in the comparison."[18]

For those who were just curious, hearing a parable from Jesus was simply a nice story; they did not really get the point. For those who were seeking truth, they could ask Jesus to explain the truth behind the parable. The meaning was no longer concealed; it was revealed.

There are two more important points to remember about parables: a parable portrays one situation like another; it is not a representation. Thus, the illustration usually refers to a single aspect of the parable or magnifies a single aspect of the message.

Finally, the story must be plausible. It must be about someone or something that could possibly occur by what the speaker or hearers believe to be possible. If the story is about a complete impossibility to either the speaker or hearers, then it would be called a fable.

Matthew 13:13
Therefore speak I to them in parables: because they seeing see not; and hearing they hear not, neither do they understand.

Matthew 13:11-17
He answered and said unto them, Because it is given unto you to know the mysteries of the kingdom of heaven, but to them it is not given.

For whosoever hath, to him shall be given, and he shall have more abundance: but whosoever hath not, from him shall be taken away even that he hath.

Therefore speak I to them in parables: because they seeing see not; and hearing they hear not, neither do they understand.

And in them is fulfilled the prophecy of Esaias, which saith, By hearing ye shall hear, and shall not understand; and seeing ye shall see, and shall not perceive:

18   Ibid

For this people's heart is waxed gross, and their ears are dull of hearing, and their eyes they have closed; lest at any time they should see with their eyes and hear with their ears, and should understand with their heart, and should be converted, and I should heal them.

But blessed are your eyes, for they see: and your ears, for they hear.

For verily I say unto you, That many prophets and righteous men have desired to see those things which ye see, and have not seen them; and to hear those things which ye hear, and have not heard them.

Chapter 19

Ten Pieces of Silver

*Either what woman having ten pieces of silver, if she lose one piece,
doth not light a candle, and sweep the house, and seek diligently till
she find it? Luke 15:8*

This record of the ten pieces of silver is yet another example of how a
little insight into eastern culture can help a western reader understand
the Bible.

In the Gospel of Luke, Jesus told a parable about a woman who had
ten pieces of silver and lost one piece. She diligently looked until she
found it. Then she did something someone today might find very odd.
She called all her friends and neighbors together so they could celebrate
with her because she found the lost piece of silver. Honestly, if my wife
lost a coin, searched all over the house, and then upon finding it called
our neighbors over for a big party, I would find that very strange.

However, in the eastern culture the ten pieces of silver were a gift from
her husband. They were not expensive, but they carried a very deep
sentimental value. It was not the only gift given to her by her husband,
but it was the most precious by far. Each coin, about the size of a
quarter, would have the coat of arms of the husband's family on one
side and usually the year the coin was made was on the other side.

On very special occasions, a woman would hang these in her hair.
Because it had such a precious and sentimental value, she was very
careful when wearing the ten pieces of silver. None of the ten pieces
could be replaced. The consequences of losing even one piece were
very harsh.

If the wife was to lose one, her husband would banish her from the
house until she found it. They believed that if she lost even one piece
of the ten, then she lost God's blessings as well.

In situations where the husband died before his wife, the ten pieces of silver were returned to her husband's family so that they could be given to another bride. She kept all the other jewelry, but the ten pieces of silver went back to his family.

After telling the parable of the woman losing and then rejoicing over the found piece of silver, Jesus made a fantastic point. Understanding the deep significance of the ten pieces of silver, his point was so very clear.

Just like a woman rejoicing over finding one of her lost pieces of silver, there is joy in heaven over one sinner who repents. God places a very high value on each and every person. When even one person accepts Christ, there is joy in the presence of the angels of God.

It reminds me of the lyrics of the song, "Amazing Grace," "I once was lost, but now am found." Since we have been "found," we have been saved from the consequences of sin by the completed work of Jesus Christ.

This parable is the second of three back-to-back parables in the Gospel of Luke; all three convey the same basic message. Perhaps consider taking the time to read all three.

Luke 15:8-10:
Either what woman having ten pieces of silver, if she lose one piece, doth not light a candle, and sweep the house, and seek diligently till she find it?

And when she hath found it, she calleth her friends and her neighbours together, saying, Rejoice with me; for I have found the piece which I had lost.

Likewise, I say unto you, there is joy in the presence of the angels of God over one sinner that repenteth.

Chapter 20

Lend Me Three Loaves

And he said unto them, Which of you shall have a friend, and shall go unto him at midnight, and say unto him, Friend, lend me three loaves;
Luke 11:5

Today, if friends from far away visit, we can generally have a pretty good idea of when they will arrive. In biblical times, however, they never really knew when someone would arrive. It could even be late at night.

Understanding their culture helps us understand a parable from Luke 11. A man woke up his neighbor at midnight because a guest of his just arrived and he had no bread to set before this weary traveler. As we have previously looked at, taking proper care of guests in that culture was extremely important, so much so that one would even wake his neighbor at midnight.

First, consider why he asked for three loaves. In our modern day, we picture a loaf of bread as either about 12 to14 inches long, sliced and rectangular or a longer, oblong shaped loaf 18 to 20 inches long. In biblical times, their bread was much different.

The bread in the Bible was round and flat like a pancake, about the size and thickness of a plate. Most people could only eat one of those loaves. A man coming in from physically working hard all day might possibly eat two. Why then, did the man in the parable ask for three?

The custom was to always serve three; to serve fewer was considered rude. It reminds me of my grandmother who always had more food set out on the table than anyone could possibly eat. This display of abundance certainly encouraged the guest to eat as much as they want, and that was the whole idea.

In the parable, the man awakened out of sleep refused to help because he said his children were in bed with him. In other words, he did not want to wake the sleeping children. Some might conjecture that the man was so poor he only had one bed.

In the biblical culture, after children were five or six years old, they slept with their grandfather. Previously to that they slept with their mother. "My children are with me in bed," is referring to their practice of the children sleeping with their grandfather, and those hearing the parable would have understood that.

In that culture, grandfathers taught the children about God and spiritual truths. At night he taught them until they fell asleep. In the morning upon waking, he asked them questions about what he taught them the night before. In a sense, he was like the priest of the family.

The reason the man actually got up and gave his friend the three loaves is often overlooked or misunderstood. Keep in mind the context in this passage is about prayer.

It very plainly says that the man did not finally get up and give him the three requested loaves because of friendship but instead because of his friend's importunity. Many misread that word, assuming it says, "opportunity," but it says, "importunity."

Importunity means shamelessness.[19] Even though it was midnight, and even though his friend refused, the man who needed bread continued to shamelessly ask, and ask, and ask. That is why right after he spoke this parable, Jesus said, "And I say unto you, Ask, and it shall be given you; seek, and ye shall find; knock, and it shall be opened unto you."

The point Jesus was making to his disciples was to continue to ask, continue to seek, and continue to knock. We ought to continue going to God in prayer as well with our requests with great persistence. Later in the Gospel of Luke, Jesus shared another parable about prayer saying to "always pray, and faint not." In other words, keep on persistently praying.

Once again, understanding the culture helps us to understand this parable and gain greater insight about prayer.

19   E.W. Bullinger, *A Critical Lexicon and Concordance to the English and Greek new Testament* (Zondervan Printing 1975), 402

Luke 11:1-10
And it came to pass, that, as he was praying in a certain place, when he ceased, one of his disciples said unto him, Lord, teach us to pray, as John also taught his disciples.

And he said unto them, When ye pray, say, Our Father which art in heaven, Hallowed be thy name. Thy kingdom come. Thy will be done, as in heaven, so in earth.

Give us day by day our daily bread.

And forgive us our sins; for we also forgive every one that is indebted to us. And lead us not into temptation; but deliver us from evil.

And he said unto them, Which of you shall have a friend, and shall go unto him at midnight, and say unto him, Friend, lend me three loaves;

For a friend of mine in his journey is come to me, and I have nothing to set before him?

And he from within shall answer and say, Trouble me not: the door is now shut, and my children are with me in bed; I cannot rise and give thee.

I say unto you, Though he will not rise and give him, because he is his friend, yet because of his importunity he will rise and give him as many as he needeth.

And I say unto you, Ask, and it shall be given you; seek, and ye shall find; knock, and it shall be opened unto you.

For every one that asketh receiveth; and he that seeketh findeth; and to him that knocketh it shall be opened.

Luke 18:1
And he spake a parable unto them to this end, that men ought always to pray, and not to faint;

Chapter 21

Devouring Widows' Houses

Woe unto you, scribes and Pharisees, hypocrites! for ye devour widows' houses, and for a pretence make long prayer: therefore ye shall receive the greater damnation. Matthew 23:14

There are several places in the Gospels where Jesus criticizes the Scribes and Pharisees. As the religious leaders of their day and time, they not only should have set the example of following God but also should have taught people rightly concerning God. In Jesus' day they did neither; thus, his criticism was justified.

One of his many comments about them was concerning widows. He said they "devoured widows' houses, and for a pretense of long prayer." Let's take a look at the culture of that time to open our eyes to what he was saying.

In the lands and times of the Bible, women did not share the same rights as men. Business matters that both women and men in the United States take for granted today were inaccessible to women back then. The limitations became quite challenging for a married woman who became a widow, especially where property was involved.

In order for a widow to conduct business affairs, she would need to decide on a trustee. She would often send a message to the Rabbi asking for help. The Rabbi, in turn, would send several men so she could choose who she wanted to handle her affairs, and many times those sent would be Scribes or Pharisees.

In our day and time this would be comparable to a group of priests, pastors, or ministers going to a widow's house. She could converse with them and then select who she thought would be best at serving her interests and conducting her business properly.

In biblical times, people looked up to the Scribes and Pharisees as "holy men" for spiritual guidance. Jesus spoke to and about them on several occasions, though never favorably. His derogatory comments showed just how far they were from being holy; he clearly pointed out that they did not represent God.

When these so called "holy men" arrived at a widow's house, they not only discussed how well they would handle her affairs, but they also prayed in front of her. Many times, it was their long and "pious" prayers that influenced the widow to legally allow one of them to be her trustee and take over her business affairs.

The devouring of her house means that he handled the affairs very dishonorably and cheated her. He made deals to profit himself, sold property, and she essentially ended up with nothing; what she had was devoured.

The contempt Jesus had for the religious leaders of his day and time is noteworthy. One certainly does not read any of that from him toward the common people or even sinners. His scathing reproof to the religious leaders was because they were supposed to be representing God; they were supposed to be conducting affairs in a godly fashion. His comments allowed those who heard to see what was really going on.

If the religious leaders of his day and time had been truly walking with and for God, they would have recognized His son in their presence. They not only refused to acknowledge who Jesus was, but they also had great hatred for him and eventually manipulated and supervised his death. They had the long-awaited Messiah, the son of God, walking right there among them, and they chose to reject him.

Jesus said that he was the way, the truth, and the life, and that no one comes to the Father but by him. In Acts 4 it says, "Neither is there salvation in any other: for there is none other name under heaven given among men, whereby we must be saved."

God's Word promises that whosoever believes in him shall not perish but have everlasting life. Salvation is a gift from God. If one confesses with the mouth the Lord Jesus and believes in his or her heart that God has raised him from the dead, that person shall be saved.

Matthew 23:14
Woe unto you, scribes and Pharisees, hypocrites! for ye devour widows' houses, and for a pretence make long prayer: therefore ye shall receive the greater damnation.

John 14:6
Jesus saith unto him, I am the way, the truth, and the life: no man cometh unto the Father, but by me.

Acts 4:12
Neither is there salvation in any other: for there is none other name under heaven given among men, whereby we must be saved.

Ephesians 2:5, 8, 9
Even when we were dead in sins, hath quickened us together with Christ, (by grace ye are saved;)

For by grace are ye saved through faith; and that not of yourselves: it is the gift of God:

Not of works, lest any man should boast.

Romans 10:9
That if thou shalt confess with thy mouth the Lord Jesus, and shalt believe in thine heart that God hath raised him from the dead, thou shalt be saved.

Chapter 22

Ten Virgins

Then shall the kingdom of heaven be likened unto ten virgins,
which took their lamps, and went forth to meet the bridegroom.
Matthew 25:1

Without an understanding of eastern marriage customs, the meaning of the record in Matthew 25 (printed below) about the five wise and five foolish virgins is a bit difficult to grasp. A little insight about weddings in biblical times sheds light on this passage. Keep in mind this parable pertains to the kingdom of heaven.

The parable begins with ten virgins taking their lamps (torches) to meet the bridegroom. The festivities would last ten days. Shortly before the wedding began, the bride's mother and father would stand outside the door of their home and wait for the arrival of the bridegroom and the ten virgins carrying their torches.

Like our modern-day bridesmaids, the ten virgins were part of the wedding party, each performing a specific task for one of the ten days. These ladies were usually relatives of the bride, and they arrived at the bride's house with their torches and oil for the torches a day before the wedding to help with the decorations. The torches were four or five feet in length.

The wedding itself would begin at midnight. Sometime before then, the virgins would take their unlit torches and oil and wait for the bridegroom at an inn at the gate of the city. When the bridegroom arrived, they lit their torches and proceeded to the bride's house, and the wedding ceremony commenced.

In the parable, all ten bridesmaids went out to meet the bridegroom at the inn. We also learn the five foolish virgins did not bring any oil for their torches. When the bridegroom finally arrived, it was time to light the torches and proceed to the bride's house.

The five foolish virgins then exclaimed they needed oil because they said their torches had gone out. That was not true. The torches were not lit until the bridegroom arrived, and the record states they did not bring any oil for their torches.

It is important to note those hearing this parable were quite familiar with wedding customs. For a virgin in the wedding party to not bring oil for her torch was indeed a very foolish thing to do.

The wise virgins preserved their oil for their own torches instead of sharing it with the foolish ones. For them to enter the house for the wedding ceremony they each needed a lit torch. They told the foolish virgins to go and buy some oil.

One might wonder about buying oil around midnight. In biblical times, weddings were considered sacred. Most shopkeepers lived at their shops or next to them, and waking a shopkeeper for something that important would be viewed as doing a service to God.

Once the entire wedding party arrived at the bride's house, the father of the bride would wash the feet of the bridegroom. Then, just at midnight, everyone would enter the house and the door was shut; no one could enter in once the door was shut.

Jesus began by saying the kingdom of heaven was like these ten virgins. At the end of the parable, he told them to watch because they did not know the day or the hour when the son of man would come.

To those hearing this parable, it would have been obvious the five virgins who did not bring oil were very foolish. Those listening may have thought, "How could they be so stupid? They knew what they were supposed to do."

The point for them, which is still true for people today, is to not be foolish. No one knows when Christ will return. It would be wise to accept Christ now in order to enter the kingdom of heaven before the door is shut.

Matthew 25:1-13

Then shall the kingdom of heaven be likened unto ten virgins, which took their lamps, and went forth to meet the bridegroom.

And five of them were wise, and five were foolish.

They that were foolish took their lamps, and took no oil with them:

But the wise took oil in their vessels with their lamps.

While the bridegroom tarried, they all slumbered and slept.

And at midnight there was a cry made, Behold, the bridegroom cometh; go ye out to meet him.

Then all those virgins arose, and trimmed their lamps.

And the foolish said unto the wise, Give us of your oil; for our lamps are gone out.

But the wise answered, saying, Not so; lest there be not enough for us and you: but go ye rather to them that sell, and buy for yourselves.

And while they went to buy, the bridegroom came; and they that were ready went in with him to the marriage: and the door was shut.

Afterward came also the other virgins, saying, Lord, Lord, open to us.

But he answered and said, Verily I say unto you, I know you not.

Watch therefore, for ye know neither the day nor the hour wherein the Son of man cometh.

Chapter 23

Wash His Feet with Tears

And, behold, a woman in the city, which was a sinner, when she knew that Jesus sat at meat in the Pharisee's house, brought an alabaster box of ointment,

And stood at his feet behind him weeping, and began to wash his feet with tears, and did wipe them with the hairs of her head, and kissed his feet, and anointed them with the ointment. Luke 7:37-38

This record in the Gospel of Luke (full account printed below) tells of a woman washing the feet of Jesus with her tears. Without understanding the customs of biblical times, one might think she was crying hard enough to produce enough tears to wash Jesus' feet. While she was indeed weeping, those were not the tears she used to wash his feet.

The woman in the record was seeking forgiveness, and she received it. In biblical times one did not go to see a spiritual man empty-handed. A gift was always brought. She brought to Jesus an alabaster box of ointment that she used to anoint his feet. She did this after washing his feet with her tears and drying his feet with her hair.

In a record in I Kings, the instructions to a woman going to see the prophet were, "Take ten loaves, and cracknels, and a cruse of honey." In another record in II Kings, a man was instructed, "Take a present in your hand, and go, meet the man of God…"

In this record in Luke 7, the alabaster box of ointment was a costly item, but it did not compare to the worth of her tears. Even though she was weeping while carrying out this act of love, the tears she washed his feet with were the tears from her tear bottle.

While not common today, keeping tears in a bottle or container has a long history including as recently as during the U.S. Civil War. In Psalm 56 David mentions the tear bottle.

The custom in biblical times was to collect tears of devotion in a container called a tear bottle. It had great significance, so much so that when a person was buried, the tear bottle was buried with him or her. They believed that any tears shed for a spiritual cause would be rewarded by God.

Thus, their tear bottles were very precious to them. If one's house was on fire, the tear bottles were saved first. It was a great sacrifice for this woman to wash Jesus' feet with the tears from her tear bottle.

Then she dried his feet with her hair. In our western culture that may sound a bit odd, but in the biblical culture, a woman's hair was her glory. She was indicating to everyone there that her glory was only good enough to wash this man's feet. In other words, she displayed great humility.

Before she anointed his feet, she kissed them. It was customary in the eastern culture to kiss each other on the forehead, crown of the head, and cheek. A kiss on the feet "was a mark of affection and of reverence. It was also the practice of supplicants, and of those who had an important request to present."[20]

This woman came to Jesus with great reverence and humility seeking forgiveness, and she received it. Meanwhile, Simon, whose house this event took place in, thought very poorly of Jesus because he did not recognize this woman as a sinner. Simon was a Pharisee, and his religious arrogance is in great contrast to Jesus' love and forgiveness for this woman.

Jesus reproved Simon for three things Simon did not do that were very common for a host to do for a guest. Simon failed to wash Jesus' feet when he arrived, he did not greet him with a kiss of respect, and he did not anoint Jesus' head with oil.

In our culture it is common to greet a guest coming into our home for dinner and perhaps offer them a drink of water. If we fail to do this, one could rightly say we are a rude host. Simon was a rude host.

After reproving Simon, Jesus said that because of this woman's love, her sins were forgiven. He told her that her faith (or believing) had saved her and to go in peace.

20   Janes M. Freeman, *Manners and Customs of the Bible* (reprinted 1972 by Logos International from original printing of Nelson and Phillips New York), 414

This woman knew she was a sinner. She went to Jesus with humility and love believing who he was and that he could offer her forgiveness. Simon only saw that she was a sinner and thought Jesus could not possibly be a prophet because he did not even recognize she was a sinner. In contrast to this hypocritical thinking, Jesus saw her heart and did what he always did, the Father's will; he forgave her.

Today, far too many people focus only on other people's sins; they preach on sin, talk about how bad sin is, and discuss how horrible sinners are. It is all too easy for someone hearing those messages to become sin-conscious and feel condemned and unworthy.

People need to hear our loving Father is a God of forgiveness. His son, Jesus Christ, paid the price for all sins, and because of that full payment, forgiveness is available to you, me, and everyone else. Perhaps instead of a message of how bad sin is, we could share a message of how great God's love and forgiveness is.

Luke 7:37-50
And, behold, a woman in the city, which was a sinner, when she knew that Jesus sat at meat in the Pharisee's house, brought an alabaster box of ointment,

And stood at his feet behind him weeping, and began to wash his feet with tears, and did wipe them with the hairs of her head, and kissed his feet, and anointed them with the ointment.

Now when the Pharisee which had bidden him saw it, he spake within himself, saying, This man, if he were a prophet, would have known who and what manner of woman this is that toucheth him: for she is a sinner.

And Jesus answering said unto him, Simon, I have somewhat to say unto thee. And he saith, Master, say on.

There was a certain creditor which had two debtors: the one owed five hundred pence, and the other fifty.

And when they had nothing to pay, he frankly forgave them both. Tell me therefore, which of them will love him most?

Simon answered and said, I suppose that he, to whom he forgave most. And he said unto him, Thou hast rightly judged.

And he turned to the woman, and said unto Simon, Seest thou this woman? I entered into thine house, thou gavest me no water for my feet: but she hath washed my feet with tears, and wiped them with the hairs of her head.

Thou gavest me no kiss: but this woman since the time I came in hath not ceased to kiss my feet.

My head with oil thou didst not anoint: but this woman hath anointed my feet with ointment.

Wherefore I say unto thee, Her sins, which are many, are forgiven; for she loved much: but to whom little is forgiven, the same loveth little.

And he said unto her, Thy sins are forgiven.

And they that sat at meat with him began to say within themselves, Who is this that forgiveth sins also?

And he said to the woman, Thy faith hath saved thee; go in peace.

I Kings 14:3
And take with thee ten loaves, and cracknels, and a cruse of honey, and go to him: he shall tell thee what shall become of the child.

II Kings 8:8
And the king said unto Hazael, Take a present in thine hand, and go, meet the man of God, and inquire of the LORD by him, saying, Shall I recover of this disease?

Psalm 56:8
Thou tellest my wanderings: put thou my tears into thy bottle: are they not in thy book?

Psalm 2:12
Kiss the Son, lest he be angry, and ye perish from the way, when his wrath is kindled but a little. Blessed are all they that put their trust in him.

I Corinthians 11:15
But if a woman have long hair, it is a glory to her: for her hair is given her for a covering.

I John 2:1 and 2
My little children, these things write I unto you, that ye sin not. And if any man sin, we have an advocate with the Father, Jesus Christ the righteous:

And he is the propitiation for our sins: and not for ours only, but also for the sins of the whole world.

Chapter 24

If Thy Right Eye Offend Thee, Pluck It Out

*And if thy right eye offend thee, pluck it out, and cast it from thee: for
it is profitable for thee that one of thy members should perish, and not
that thy whole body should be cast into hell.*

*And if thy right hand offend thee, cut it off, and cast it from thee: for
it is profitable for thee that one of thy members should perish, and not
that thy whole body should be cast into hell. Matthew 5:29, 30*

Understanding idioms used in the Bible can be very helpful in not taking
something that is meant figuratively in a literal sense. In the Scripture
above, Jesus said to pluck out one's right eye. Did he mean it literally?
That sounds painful and drastic, yet Jesus said to do it.

Then he said, "And if thy right hand offend thee, cut it off, and cast it
from thee." Again, this would be painful and drastic, but rest assured
these are idioms.

An idiom is a style of speaking peculiar to a people or language.[21] It is a
combination of words that has a figurative meaning specific to a people,
community, or class. An idiom's figurative meaning is separate from
the literal meaning. Idioms are present in every language and culture.

For example, if someone is upset and crying, someone might say, "She
is crying her eyes out." That is not a literal statement. It is figurative;
it is an idiom.

In biblical times, "right eye offend thee," was an idiomatic way of saying
not to be envious or jealous. The point Jesus was making was to avoid
envy and jealousy. When he said, "pluck it out," those present understood
he was telling them to control their thinking so as not to be envious or
jealous. Using this idiom brought great emphasis to that point.

---

21   Random House Webster's College Dictionary, 2nd Revised and Updated ed., s.v.
"idiom."

When he followed with, "right hand offend thee," he meant to not steal. He told them to cut it off to show the degree of determination they should have to not steal. Cutting off the right hand that offends is to absolutely determine they will not steal.

Having an understanding of idioms used in the Bible helps us understand and follow what Jesus taught. We should not be envious or jealous, and we should not steal. In our culture, we might use the idiom, "Cut it out," to tell someone to stop his or her negative behavior.

Idioms are wonderful grammatical figures of speech that illuminate and emphasize what is written or spoken, and God employed many of them in His written Word. Understanding the idioms Jesus used helps us clearly see the intended meaning.

Matthew 5:29.30
And if thy right eye offend thee, pluck it out, and cast it from thee: for it is profitable for thee that one of thy members should perish, and not that thy whole body should be cast into hell.

And if thy right hand offend thee, cut it off, and cast it from thee: for it is profitable for thee that one of thy members should perish, and not that thy whole body should be cast into hell.

Chapter 25

Turn the Other Cheek

But I say unto you, That ye resist not evil: but whosoever shall smite thee on thy right cheek, turn to him the other also. Matthew 5:39

In the context of this verse from Matthew's Gospel, Jesus Christ was teaching that although the Law instructed in Exodus 21:24 to give an eye for an eye, whosoever shall smite a person on his right cheek, should turn to him the other cheek also. From this verse the phrase was coined, "turn the other cheek."

Some take this verse literally and believe it means physical abuse should be endured. The Greek word translated "smite" in this verse does not necessarily mean to inflict pain or injury. It can also mean to simply touch someone.

It is most helpful to remember the words Jesus spoke and employed were well known and understood by the people he spoke to. His message was new, but the words and phrases he used to convey that message were not new.

In biblical culture, one of the greatest insults was for someone to touch another's cheek with one's hand. Bishop Pillai explains, "It should have been translated 'touch' in this verse, not 'smite.' In the East, to touch the cheek of another man is a very great insult."[22]

This is what Jesus meant when he said, "whosoever shall smith thee on thy right cheek, turn to him the other also." If someone did touch another's cheek, it would be a very great insult, but the Master's message was clear: do not retaliate; do not respond to an insult with another insult. Even though it may be humiliating, let them touch the cheek on the other side, too. He most certainly was not saying if someone smacked a person in the face that he should just endure further abuse by giving him the other cheek to hit as well.

---

22   Bishop K.C. Pillai, "Matthew" retrieved from http://www.biblecustoms.org/bishop-kc-pillai/old-and-new-testament-orientalisms/matthew

However, if someone does insult another, by the grace of God that person can "turn the other cheek," and bless them instead of retaliating against them. The Bible teaches, "Bless them which persecute you: bless, and curse not."

Matthew 5:39
But I say unto you, That ye resist not evil: but whosoever shall smite thee on thy right cheek, turn to him the other also.

Romans 12:14
Bless them which persecute you: bless, and curse not.

Chapter 26

Blind Bartimaeus

And they came to Jericho: and as he went out of Jericho with his disciples and a great number of people, blind Bartimaeus, the son of Timaeus, sat by the highway side begging. Mark 10:46

There is a record in the Gospel of Mark about a blind man receiving healing from Jesus. The man's name was Bartimaeus. There are some very interesting details in the record that are often overlooked due to misunderstandings of the eastern culture.

In our modern world, it is common to see people on various corners holding up signs asking for help. It is assumed these people are begging for money. In the lands and times of the Bible, there were people begging who did not have a financial need. When we read about someone begging in the Scriptures, we cannot automatically assume they were begging for money.

In biblical times, there were three main areas where it was common to find beggars: at the gate of a temple, holy rivers or other bodies of water, and on the highway or public thoroughfares. The latter is where Bartimaeus was begging when he called out to Jesus.

People who did not have a financial need would beg for their healing. We understand from reading this account in the Gospel of Mark that Bartimaeus was blind, but was he poor?

The Scriptural account says, "Blind Bartimaeus, the son of Timaeus, sat by the highway side begging." If he were begging out of financial need, in other words, poor and destitute with no family to help or assist, there would have been no mention of his lineage; his father's name would not have been given. This is the first of two indicators Bartimaeus was on the highway begging for healing and not for money.

People in the lands and times of the Bible did this to obtain mercy from God. They became as lowly as a beggar in a public place, humbling themselves, hoping that a holy man might pass by, and they could receive healing.

When Bartimaeus heard that Jesus of Nazareth was passing by, he cried out saying, "Jesus thou son of David, have mercy on me." Those around him told him to be quiet. Instead, he kept crying out for Jesus to have mercy on him.

Jesus stopped and called for the man. Those who had been telling him to be quiet started telling him, "Be of good comfort, rise; he calls you."

The Scriptural account next includes another important detail that is often overlooked but has great significance. "And he, casting away his garment, rose, and came to Jesus." No one told him to cast away his garment. Why did he do that?

The garment he cast away was his robe. Those who begged for healing as opposed to financial need often wore their robes. Seeing someone begging in a robe instead of rags would be an obvious indication the person was begging for healing.

A person's robe indicated his status, his authority, his position in the community, his standing, as well as his dignity. When Jesus called for Bartimaeus, he cast away his robe and went to Jesus empty. He came before Christ empty of all pride, dignity, standing, and status; he stood before him with great humility to obtain mercy.

It is inspiring to see Bartimaeus choosing to lay aside all his pride. No one told him he should do that. It was his choice.

The Bible teaches that God resists the proud but gives grace to the humble. Bartimaeus going before Jesus, empty of all pride, is a great example of humility.

We can also choose to empty ourselves of pride. We can approach our loving Father with humility. We can choose to get rid of our ego and self-righteous bravado. We can approach our God with the confidence and open entrance we have as His children and with the humbleness of once blind, but later healed, Bartimaeus.

Mark 10:46-52
And they came to Jericho: and as he went out of Jericho with his disciples and a great number of people, blind Bartimaeus, the son of Timaeus, sat by the highway side begging.

And when he heard that it was Jesus of Nazareth, he began to cry out, and say, Jesus, thou Son of David, have mercy on me.

And many charged him that he should hold his peace: but he cried the more a great deal, Thou Son of David, have mercy on me.

And Jesus stood still, and commanded him to be called. And they call the blind man, saying unto him, Be of good comfort, rise; he calls you.

And he, casting away his garment, rose, and came to Jesus.

And Jesus answered and said unto him, What will you that I should do unto you? The blind man said unto him, Lord, that I might receive my sight.

And Jesus said unto him, Go thy way; thy faith hath made thee whole. And immediately he received his sight, and followed Jesus in the way.

I Peter 5:5b-7
For God resisteth the proud, and giveth grace to the humble.

Humble yourselves therefore under the mighty hand of God, that he may exalt you in due time:

Casting all your care upon him; for he careth for you.

Chapter 27

A Reed Shaken with the Wind

And as they departed, Jesus began to say unto the multitudes concerning John, What went ye out into the wilderness to see? A reed shaken with the wind? Matthew 11:7

Jesus Christ asked a very pointed question to those who had gone out into the wilderness to hear John the Baptist teach. He asked them if they went out to see "a reed shaken by the wind."

This phrasing is quite foreign to the western way of speaking. Understanding what life was like in biblical times sheds light on this verse.

The reeds Jesus spoke of were in the sugar cane family and grew wild. They were often used to make flutes. They would generally grow four to five feet tall.

During the heat of the day, they would droop with their tops falling all the way to the ground, but when the cool evening winds came, they would all rise back up straight and tall. The people thought this was a beautiful sight to see and would often go out to watch them rise again.

Jesus asked those who had gone out to see John the Baptist, "What did you go out to see? A reed shaken by the wind?" In other words, he was asking if they went out to see and hear John's message or if they went out to watch the reeds.

Obviously, there was nothing wrong with watching the reeds. It was a beautiful sight to see. However, for those who went out specifically to see John, Jesus wanted to know what they were focused on. Were they listening to what John had to say, or were they distracted?

There are many old churches around the world that are very beautiful. I have personally visited some of the most famous ones in Spain, Italy, and Greece. The beauty and ornate grandeur of some of those churches is often breathtaking. Many modern churches are beautiful as well.

Wherever one goes to hear God's Word, the beautiful decorations are not what are most important. It is not how big the choir is. It is not even how many people attend. If God's Word is being taught, that is what is most important.

One may call to mind some of the simple surroundings when Jesus taught God's Word, including walking on the road to Emmaus. All the trappings and embellishments may be nice, but the Word of God can be taught without any of those things. It is the message we should be going to hear.

Matthew 11:7
And as they departed, Jesus began to say unto the multitudes concerning John, What went ye out into the wilderness to see? A reed shaken with the wind?

Luke 7:24
And when the messengers of John were departed, he began to speak unto the people concerning John, What went ye out into the wilderness for to see? A reed shaken with the wind?

Chapter 28

Bread, Fish, and an Egg

If a son shall ask bread of any of you that is a father,
will he give him a stone? or if he ask a fish,
will he for a fish give him a serpent?

Or if he shall ask an egg, will he offer him a scorpion?
Luke 11:11 and 12

Jesus Christ taught about prayer many times. On one occasion, making a very important point, he asked three rhetorical questions. One question would have been sufficient, but in asking three questions the point would be hard to miss.

However, without understanding the eastern culture, one could not only miss the point, but also wonder what in the world Jesus was talking about. Not having knowledge of certain norms and customs in biblical times makes this record puzzling.

This is true in any culture. Suppose someone completely unfamiliar with the culture in the United States heard expressions like, "For supper I had a hot dog," or, "It was hard to sleep because it was raining cats and dogs." They might very well be confused.

Jesus asked those who were listening three questions. The first was: if a son asked his father for bread, would a father instead give his son a stone? The second question was: if a son asked his father for a fish, would his father then give him a serpent instead? The final question was: if a son asked his father for an egg, would the father in turn give the son a scorpion?

To the eastern mind, this is easily understood; those three rhetorical questions would be immediately answered with a resounding, "No!" To our western minds, however, it seems rather odd.

We might think, "What kind of father could either be that stupid or that cruel to give his child those items instead of what the child asked for?" Yet, once we understand bread, fish, and scorpions in biblical times, the meaning clearly unfolds.

As we have seen before, bread in biblical times was quite different than the bread we have today. The cooked bread, round and flat, was placed on a stone that was about the same size as the bread. They would stack the bread one on top of another, and then another stone would be placed on top to protect the bread.

The butter-like substance used in cooking the bread would soak into the stones, and at a glance, the stones might even look like the bread. Still, no father would ever be so foolish as to mistake a stone for bread and give it to his son who asked him for bread.

In the eastern lands there are some water serpents that look similar to fish. A person unfamiliar with both fish and water serpents could easily mistake one for the other. A loving father concerned about his family would certainly make sure that there was no mistake. If his son asked for a fish, that is what a good loving father would give him.

The body of a scorpion is shaped very similarly to an egg. The white scorpion in the east could possibly be mistaken for an egg. I once read that if one were to cut open the body of a white scorpion, the inside would be white and yellow. Suffice it to say, I have not tried this personally.

Perhaps a young child might not recognize the difference between the body of a scorpion and an egg, but what father would not? What father, whose son asked for an egg, would ever give his son a scorpion instead?

The answer to all three of these rhetorical questions is a resounding, "No!"

After asking those three questions, Jesus went on to say, "If you then, being evil, know how to give good gifts unto your children: how much more shall your heavenly Father give the Holy Spirit to them that ask him?" Similarly, Matthew's Gospel says, "If you then, being evil, know how to give good gifts unto your children, how much more shall your Father which is in heaven give good things to them that ask him?"

The reference to "being evil" simply means that we are not perfect. We do not always do the right things. God, however, is perfect.

Even though we are not perfect, we would never give one of our children a stone instead of bread, a serpent instead of a fish, or a scorpion instead of an egg. Thus, if we as imperfect people can still give good gifts to our children, how much more will our heavenly Father give us good things, including the holy spirit, when we ask Him?

In our culture we could very easily understand if the questions would have been about sweets. If our children asked us for some candy, would we give them marbles instead? If they asked for some marshmallows, would we give them cotton balls instead? We certainly would not.

Jesus Christ was teaching about prayer. He was communicating to them about the heavenly Father answering prayers. By asking these rhetorical questions, it became very clear to those listening that God is not going to respond to requests with something inferior. He is not going to answer requests with something that would be harmful.

We can confidently go to God in prayer. We can be assured knowing He wants to answer our prayers. We can truly have confidence in our heavenly Father because He goes way beyond any human dad— infinitely more.

Luke 11:11-13
If a son shall ask bread of any of you that is a father, will he give him a stone? or if he ask a fish, will he for a fish give him a serpent?

Or if he shall ask an egg, will he offer him a scorpion?

If ye then, being evil, know how to give good gifts unto your children: how much more shall your heavenly Father give the Holy Spirit to them that ask him?

Matthew 7:7-11
Ask, and it shall be given you; seek, and ye shall find; knock, and it shall be opened unto you:

For every one that asketh receiveth; and he that seeketh findeth; and to him that knocketh it shall be opened.

Or what man is there of you, whom if his son ask bread, will he give him a stone?

Or if he ask a fish, will he give him a serpent?

If ye then, being evil, know how to give good gifts unto your children, how much more shall your Father which is in heaven give good things to them that ask him?

Chapter 29

Fish with Money in Its Mouth

Notwithstanding, lest we should offend them, go thou to the sea,
and cast an hook, and take up the fish that first cometh up;
and when thou hast opened his mouth, thou shalt find a piece of
money: that take, and give unto them for me and thee. Matthew 17:27

The verse above relates to an interesting event in the gospel of Matthew in which Jesus sends Peter, a very experienced fisherman, to catch a fish. Jesus told Peter that the first fish he caught would have money in the fish's mouth, and they would use that money to pay the tribute tax.

Some may wonder how there could be money in a fish's mouth. Some say God, by way of a miracle, put some money in that fish's mouth. Understanding the eastern culture helps us to understand what really happened.

In his work, *The Acceptable Year of the Lord*, Rev. Cummins explains, "Certain species of fish jump at glittering objects thrown into the water such as silver coins. One such fish may have been the kind of fish that Peter was to catch. That the first fish which Peter was to catch would have a coin in its mouth would have been a miracle."[23]

Bishop Pillai said this fish is called the Musht. He provides, "It is about six inches long. It has a large head and a bag under its mouth. The Musht picks up coins of gold and silver, jewelry, diamonds, and rubies – anything that sparkles in the water – and keeps them in the bag. This particular fish is very tricky and difficult to hook. A man might fish for twenty-five years and never catch one, or he might get one on his first trip."[24]

Today there is a tradition of throwing coins into a fountain for good luck. Perhaps the most famous is the Trevi Fountain in Rome. When I

23 Walter J. Cummins, *The Acceptable Year of the Lord* (Scripture Consulting Franklin, Ohio, 2005), *339*
24 Bishop K.C. Pillai, *Orientalisms of the Bible* (Mor-Mac Publishing Company, Inc. 1969), *43*

saw it several years ago, there were a vast amount of coins in there. In fact, the tour guide said approximately 3,000 euros are thrown into the fountain every day.

Many believe this tradition of throwing coins into fountains goes back hundreds of years when offerings were thrown into "holy waters." In biblical times, offerings to God were taken very seriously. There were those who wanted to give an offering but did not want to receive any recognition for it. Many believed that if praise was received from men, then the reward was received right then in the form of recognition. However, what they really wanted was to receive their reward in the next world.

To keep it private, many would throw their offerings into the waters. Throwing their offerings into what were considered "holy waters" would be best. Although, depending on where one lived, any water might do.

In the biblical account we are considering, Jesus told Peter to go to the sea, cast in a hook, and take the first fish that came up. He went on to tell him that when he opened the fish's mouth he would find a piece of money. This must have been exciting for Peter. He was an experienced fisherman. He knew it was possible for this type of fish to have a coin. He also knew it was rare to catch one that had a coin.

The miracle was not the fish having a coin. The miracle was that it was the first fish Peter caught. Can you imagine him there all afternoon on the shore casting in his hook, catching a fish, checking for a coin, and finding nothing?

When Jesus sent him, Peter did not argue. He did not tell Jesus the odds of it happening. He did not doubt. He simply believed what Jesus told him.

We too can have confidence in God's promises. We can accept that what God has promised us is true. We do not need to doubt, we just need to believe that He can and will supply all our needs.

Matthew 17:24-27
And when they were come to Capernaum, they that received tribute money came to Peter, and said, Doth not your master pay tribute?

He saith, Yes. And when he was come into the house, Jesus prevented him, saying, What thinkest thou, Simon? of whom do the kings of the earth take custom or tribute? of their own children, or of strangers?

Peter saith unto him, Of strangers. Jesus saith unto him, Then are the children free.

Notwithstanding, lest we should offend them, go thou to the sea, and cast an hook, and take up the fish that first cometh up; and when thou hast opened his mouth, thou shalt find a piece of money: that take, and give unto them for me and thee.

Philippians 4:19
But my God shall supply all your needs according to his riches in Glory by Christ Jesus.

Chapter 30

Many Are Called, but Few Are Chosen

For many are called, but few are chosen. Matthew 22:14

The verse above is from a parable Jesus spoke about a wedding (complete account printed below). A guest who was improperly dressed at the wedding was kicked out. In the parable, we learn this wedding was the marriage of a king's son. This is the key to understanding this parable.

In biblical times, affluent people owned what is referred to as wedding garments or wedding robes. This attire for weddings indicated a person's social standing. More affluent people wore elaborate decorations on their wedding garments. Many times, this clothing was passed down in the family.

Sometimes weddings in our western culture today do not specify a dress code. I have officiated at weddings where some male guests did not wear a coat or a tie. I have even observed people attending explicitly stated formal weddings who were dressed quite informally. However, I have never seen anyone escorted out of a wedding for improper attire as was the case in this parable.

In biblical times, they attended weddings wearing their wedding robes. In this parable, there was a man who was attending without the proper wedding garment. Some might argue that perhaps this man could not afford the proper attire for the wedding. They would say, "Well at least he showed up for the wedding. Why was he escorted out?"

In those times, if a person was invited to a wedding given by a king for the marriage of one of his children, one did not wear his or her own wedding robe. Attending that marriage with one's own wedding robe would be a great insult because the king provided the wedding garments for all of the guests.

The king would make careful arrangements to see that all of the guests were given a wedding robe for the occasion. The garments would be delivered to each guest. Everyone who attended would then be wearing the attire provided for them by the king. Thus, the guests did not come showing their own social standing, wealth, or prestige. Instead, they were showing the king's power and prestige.

Those hearing Jesus speak this parable understood this man was not too poor to acquire a proper garment. They recognized this was not a mistake or an oversight but a deliberate act by the man in refusing what the king provided. They knew why the king ordered him to be thrown out of the wedding.

The last verse of the parable is often misunderstood. It reads, "For many are called, but few are chosen."

If one is "called" to a wedding, then that person has been invited. It would be better understood as, "Many are invited..." Many are invited, but few have chosen to accept the invitation and put on the robe provided them.

The king was not unfair or cruel. He had extended the invitation to the man and provided the robe for him. The man refused to wear the robe, which was an insult to the king. The choosing was whether the man would wear the robe the king provided. It was a free will decision by that man to accept the invitation and to wear the robe.

The chosen are those who choose to accept what God has offered. Otherwise, many would be called or invited, and then God would simply pick and choose who gets to stay and who must leave. Some may think that is the way God operates, but if that was true, then we would have no free will to decide. God never takes away a person's free will.

This is a parable about the kingdom of heaven. The choosing is by the individual, whether he is going to accept what God has extended in Christ or not. The choice is up to the individual. A person cannot earn his or her own righteousness; it is freely given because of the work of Christ.

It is not about good works. Doing one's own works to become righteous before God is refusing the righteousness He has already freely made available through the completed work of Christ. Few choose to accept both the invitation and all that God has freely extended in Christ.

Be one of the few. Make the choice. Accept God's invitation that is to all of mankind. Accept His righteousness, which is freely given through the completed work of Christ.

Matthew 22:1-14

And Jesus answered and spoke unto them again by parables, and said,

The kingdom of heaven is like unto a certain king, which made a marriage for his son,

And sent forth his servants to call them that were bidden to the wedding: and they would not come.

Again, he sent forth other servants, saying, Tell them which are bidden, Behold, I have prepared my dinner: my oxen and my fatlings are killed, and all things are ready: come unto the marriage.

But they made light of it, and went their ways, one to his farm, another to his merchandise:

And the remnant took his servants, and entreated them spitefully, and slew them.

But when the king heard thereof, he was wroth: and he sent forth his armies, and destroyed those murderers, and burned up their city.

Then said he to his servants, The wedding is ready, but they which were bidden were not worthy.

Go ye therefore into the highways, and as many as ye shall find, bid to the marriage.

So those servants went out into the highways, and gathered together all as many as they found, both bad and good: and the wedding was furnished with guests.

And when the king came in to see the guests, he saw there a man which had not on a wedding garment:

And he said unto him, Friend, how came you in hither not having a wedding garment? And he was speechless.

Then said the king to the servants, Bind him hand and foot, and take him away, and cast him into outer darkness; there shall be weeping and gnashing of teeth.

For many are called, but few are chosen.

Romans 3:22
Even the righteousness of God which is by faith of Jesus Christ unto all and upon all them that believe: for there is no difference:

Ephesians 2:8 and 9
For by grace are ye saved through faith; and that not of yourselves: it is the gift of God:

Not of works, lest any man should boast.

Chapter 31

Came to Jesus by Night

The same came to Jesus by night, and said unto him,
Rabbi, we know that thou art a teacher come from God:
for no man can do these miracles that thou doest,
except God be with him. John 3:2

Many people are familiar with this record from John's Gospel of Nicodemus going to see Jesus at night. Some have speculated he used the cover of darkness so no one would know he had been with Jesus. Understanding the culture of biblical times helps us discern why he went to see Jesus at night.

Nicodemus was a Pharisee and a member of the Sanhedrin. The Sanhedrin was the supreme council in ancient Israel. Nicodemus was also a Pharisee. The Pharisees were a Jewish sect noted for their strict observance of rites and ceremonies of the written law and for insistence on the validity of their own oral traditions concerning the law. On many occasions in the Gospels, Jesus directly confronted the Pharisees for their lack of believing the Scriptures and their hypocrisy.

In biblical culture, after sunset was the time for philosophical discussions. People sought holy men in the evening to discuss deep issues. The Bible never says Nicodemus went at night because he was afraid; he was simply acting according to his cultural norm and seeking answers.

It is interesting that Nicodemus is mentioned in two other places in John's Gospel. After this visit, he is mentioned as objecting to the chief priests and others judging Jesus without a trial. The third mention of this man is in carrying out Jesus' proper Jewish burial. In all three occurrences, the same phrase is used: "came to Jesus by night."

It is remarkable to consider what Nicodemus learned when he came to Jesus by night. Scripture records Jesus speaking to him about being "born again" or born from above—another birth. Today we often reference what Jesus explained to Nicodemus as being the new birth.

We do not know what more he spoke to Nicodemus that night. We only know what is recorded in John's Gospel. What is recorded is electrifying. While others are recorded as going to Jesus with ulterior motives, Nicodemus was there to learn.

I am impressed with Nicodemus because he chose not to follow the crowd. Most of his fellow Pharisees hated Jesus and his fellow Sanhedrin council members condemned him to death. It took courage to not be in step with his colleagues when they were following the wrong path.

It is easy to follow the crowd. Anyone can be swayed by the actions of their friends and popular opinions of the day, but just like Nicodemus, we each choose the paths we take. We are responsible for our choices and subsequent actions. Choose wisely. Nicodemus did.

John 3:1-12
There was a man of the Pharisees, named Nicodemus, a ruler of the Jews:

The same came to Jesus by night, and said unto him, Rabbi, we know that thou art a teacher come from God: for no man can do these miracles that thou doest, except God be with him.

Jesus answered and said unto him, Verily, verily, I say unto thee, Except a man be born again, he cannot see the kingdom of God.

Nicodemus saith unto him, How can a man be born when he is old? can he enter the second time into his mother's womb, and be born?

Jesus answered, Verily, verily, I say unto thee, Except a man be born of water and of the Spirit, he cannot enter into the kingdom of God.

That which is born of the flesh is flesh; and that which is born of the Spirit is spirit.

Marvel not that I said unto thee, Ye must be born again.

The wind bloweth where it listeth, and thou hearest the sound thereof, but canst not tell whence it cometh, and whither it goeth: so is every one that is born of the Spirit.

Nicodemus answered and said unto him, How can these things be?

Jesus answered and said unto him, Art thou a master of Israel, and knowest not these things?

Verily, verily, I say unto thee, We speak that we do know, and testify that we have seen; and ye receive not our witness.

If I have told you earthly things, and ye believe not, how shall ye believe, if I tell you of heavenly things?

John 7:40-53
Many of the people therefore, when they heard this saying, said, Of a truth this is the Prophet.Others said, This is the Christ. But some said, Shall Christ come out of Galilee?

Hath not the scripture said, That Christ cometh of the seed of David, and out of the town of Bethlehem, where David was?

So there was a division among the people because of him.

And some of them would have taken him; but no man laid hands on him.

Then came the officers to the chief priests and Pharisees; and they said unto them, Why have ye not brought him?

The officers answered, Never man spake like this man.

Then answered them the Pharisees, Are ye also deceived?

Have any of the rulers or of the Pharisees believed on him?

But this people who knoweth not the law are cursed.

Nicodemus saith unto them, (he that came to Jesus by night, being one of them,)

Doth our law judge any man, before it hear him, and know what he doeth?

They answered and said unto him, Art thou also of Galilee? Search, and look: for out of Galilee ariseth no prophet.

And every man went unto his own house.

John 19:39-40
And there came also Nicodemus, which at the first came to Jesus by night, and brought a mixture of myrrh and aloes, about an hundred pound weight.

Then took they the body of Jesus, and wound it in linen clothes with the spices, as the manner of the Jews is to bury.

Chapter 32

The Woman at the Well

Now Jacob's well was there. Jesus therefore, being wearied with his journey, sat thus on the well: and it was about the sixth hour.

There cometh a woman of Samaria to draw water: Jesus saith unto her, Give me to drink. John 4:6, 7

There are great truths recorded in John 4 (complete record noted below) when Jesus arrived at Sychar and talked with a woman at the well. Once again, understanding some of the customs of that day and time further enhances this familiar incident and provides great insight.

Jesus was traveling north from Judea to Galilee, and he stopped in a city in Samaria. However, Judeans traveling in that part of the country would often purposely travel greater distances to avoid going through Samaria. Jesus, who always did the will of his Father, did not avoid Samaria on this trip.

After Israel (the northern ten tribes) was taken into captivity by the Assyrians, the people who remained in Samaria intermingled with people the Assyrians brought into the Samaritan area from other lands. As a result, both the Galileans and Judeans looked down upon the Samaritans for not being full-blooded Jews. For this reason, the Samaritans were not allowed to help in rebuilding the Temple.

The Samaritans were despised by the Judeans. Judeans did everything they could to avoid any dealings with Samaritans. This sheds some interesting light on a very familiar parable Jesus told, referred to by many as the parable of the Good Samaritan.

Jesus and his disciples arrived at Sychar in Samaria around noon. He sent them to town to get food. He was tired and sat on the well, and a woman came along with her water pot to draw water.

Jesus asked her for a drink. She, being a Samaritan, recognized Jesus as a Galilean, and asked him why he would ask her for a drink of water. Jesus then began to speak to her about living water.

In the culture of the lands and times of the Bible, it was acceptable to ask a woman for water but not to have a conversation with her. However, this was a Samaritan woman, so a Judean would normally not even ask for water.

When asked for water in that culture, a woman would comply, but she would not engage in a conversation. Yet, this woman initiated the conversation when she asked Jesus why he, a Jew, was asking water from a Samaritan woman. The conversation that followed was astounding.

In the middle of the conversation, Jesus asked her to go call her husband. She answered that she had no husband. Jesus said she answered correctly because she had five husbands previously, and the current man in her life was not her husband.

It is not profitable for one to assume or speculate that this woman had been divorced five times. It is possible that her five previous husbands died. God's Word does not tell us either way. Furthermore, unlike the Judeans, the Samaritans had a custom of courting. It was possible that was the situation with the man she was seeing whom Jesus indicated was not her husband.

From reading the entire record, it is obvious this woman did not have a disreputable reputation as some have speculated. On the contrary, she must have had considerable credibility because when she left speaking with Jesus and went into town, several people not only listened to what she told them about Jesus, but they also came back with her to see Jesus.

Jesus knew some information about this woman because God, by way of His spirit in Jesus, revealed it to him. His response clearly indicated to the woman that he was a prophet, and she told him so.

She asked Jesus some pertinent questions. She wanted to know who was worshiping correctly: the Samaritans or the Judeans. Jesus answered by telling her the days were soon coming when the true worshipers would worship God by way of the spirit.

He further explained to her that God was spirit and that they who worship Him must worship Him truthfully by way of the spirit. When she next asked about the coming Messiah, he told her plainly that he was, in fact, the Messiah!

At this point in the record, the disciples returned, quite curious as to why Jesus was talking to this Samaritan woman. The woman left her water pot and headed to town to tell everyone she knew. Leaving her water pot behind was very significant.

In that culture, a woman would never leave her water pot behind. It was not expensive as it was just a clay pot, but it had great sentimental value. To leave behind a water pot was equal to forsaking God. One would be ostracized because the action indicated a lack of respect for God.

At that moment in time, after realizing who she was talking to, the consequences of breaking her custom no longer mattered. She had just met the long-awaited Messiah face to face! She went into town with a very exciting message and brought a crowd back with her.

The Samaritans asked Jesus Christ to stay with them, and he stayed for two days. What a great blessing for those Samaritans because Jesus did the will of the Father and traveled into Samaria. One can only wonder what Jesus shared with the Samaritans during those two days.

This record is very interesting when we understand the culture of the day. The woman broke custom. Jesus broke custom. Yet, God is no respecter of persons. Salvation is by God's grace, not works. God so loved the world, that He gave His only begotten Son, that whosoever believes in him would not perish, but have everlasting life.

John 4:3-43
He left Judaea, and departed again into Galilee.

And he must needs go through Samaria.

Then cometh he to a city of Samaria, which is called Sychar, near to the parcel of ground that Jacob gave to his son Joseph.

Now Jacob's well was there. Jesus therefore, being wearied with his journey, sat thus on the well: and it was about the sixth hour.

There cometh a woman of Samaria to draw water: Jesus saith unto her, Give me to drink.

(For his disciples were gone away unto the city to buy meat.)

Then saith the woman of Samaria unto him, How is it that thou, being a Jew, askest drink of me, which am a woman of Samaria? for the Jews have no dealings with the Samaritans.

Jesus answered and said unto her, If thou knewest the gift of God, and who it is that saith to thee, Give me to drink; thou wouldest have asked of him, and he would have given thee living water.

The woman saith unto him, Sir, thou hast nothing to draw with, and the well is deep: from whence then hast thou that living water?

Art thou greater than our father Jacob, which gave us the well, and drank thereof himself, and his children, and his cattle?

Jesus answered and said unto her, Whosoever drinketh of this water shall thirst again:

But whosoever drinketh of the water that I shall give him shall never thirst; but the water that I shall give him shall be in him a well of water springing up into everlasting life.

The woman saith unto him, Sir, give me this water, that I thirst not, neither come hither to draw.

Jesus saith unto her, Go, call thy husband, and come hither.

The woman answered and said, I have no husband. Jesus said unto her, Thou hast well said, I have no husband:

For thou hast had five husbands; and he whom thou now hast is not thy husband: in that saidst thou truly.

The woman saith unto him, Sir, I perceive that thou art a prophet.

Our fathers worshipped in this mountain; and ye say, that in Jerusalem is the place where men ought to worship.

Jesus saith unto her, Woman, believe me, the hour cometh, when ye shall neither in this mountain, nor yet at Jerusalem, worship the Father.

Ye worship ye know not what: we know what we worship: for salvation is of the Jews.

But the hour cometh, and now is, when the true worshippers shall worship the Father in spirit and in truth: for the Father seeketh such to worship him.

God is a Spirit: and they that worship him must worship him in spirit and in truth.

The woman saith unto him, I know that Messias cometh, which is called Christ: when he is come, he will tell us all things.

Jesus saith unto her, I that speak unto thee am he.

And upon this came his disciples, and marvelled that he talked with the woman: yet no man said, What seekest thou? or, Why talkest thou with her?

The woman then left her waterpot, and went her way into the city, and saith to the men,

Come, see a man, which told me all things that ever I did: is not this the Christ?

Then they went out of the city, and came unto him.

In the mean while his disciples prayed him, saying, Master, eat.

But he said unto them, I have meat to eat that ye know not of.

Therefore said the disciples one to another, Hath any man brought him ought to eat?

Jesus saith unto them, My meat is to do the will of him that sent me, and to finish his work.

Say not ye, There are yet four months, and then cometh harvest? behold, I say unto you, Lift up your eyes, and look on the fields; for they are white already to harvest.

And he that reapeth receiveth wages, and gathereth fruit unto life eternal: that both he that soweth and he that reapeth may rejoice together.

And herein is that saying true, One soweth, and another reapeth.

I sent you to reap that whereon ye bestowed no labour: other men laboured, and ye are entered into their labours.

And many of the Samaritans of that city believed on him for the saying of the woman, which testified, He told me all that ever I did.

So when the Samaritans were come unto him, they besought him that he would tarry with them: and he abode there two days.

And many more believed because of his own word;

And said unto the woman, Now we believe, not because of thy saying: for we have heard him ourselves, and know that this is indeed the Christ, the Saviour of the world.

Now after two days he departed thence, and went into Galilee.

Acts 10:34
Then Peter opened his mouth, and said, Of a truth I perceive that God is no respecter of persons:

Ephesians 2:8 and 9
For by grace are ye saved through faith; and that not of yourselves: it is the gift of God:

Not of works, lest any man should boast.

John 3:16
For God so loved the world, that he gave his only begotten Son, that whosoever believeth in him should not perish, but have everlasting life.

Chapter 33

Mustard Seed and Sycamine Tree

And the apostles said unto the Lord, increase our faith.

And the Lord said, If ye had faith as a grain of mustard seed,
ye might say unto this sycamine tree, be thou plucked up by the root,
and be thou planted in the sea; and it should obey you.
Luke 17:5 and 6

In answering his disciples request about how to increase their faith, Jesus gave them quite an enlightening answer. Concerning increasing their faith, or increasing their believing, he told them if they had faith the size of a mustard seed they could tell a sycamine tree to come up by the roots and plant itself in the sea, and the tree would obey.

In his answer he referenced a mustard seed and a sycamine tree. The mustard seed is one of the smallest of all seeds, yet it has potential to grow into a great mustard tree. The disciples were concerned about increasing their faith so they could do more or produce more. Jesus said all that was needed was a tiny seed's worth.

He was teaching them that when it comes to faith, or believing, it is not the size or amount that matters. Rather, one either believes or does not believe. When one does believe, the results are tremendous—big enough to uproot and replant a sycamine tree.

The sycamine tree mentioned here is the wild fig tree. Although it produces fruit usually six times a year, most people do not eat the fruit because the figs are very bitter. What is interesting is that although the sycamine tree is small, it has an enormous root system. The roots of this tree spread so wide and deep that even today with modern machinery it is impossible to pull out a sycamine tree without leaving some of the roots behind.

Yet, Jesus said to his disciples if they had faith, or believing, the size of a mustard seed, they would be able to tell a sycamine tree to be plucked out by the roots and plant itself in the sea. The smallest amount of believing could remove this bitter fruit tree with all of its extensive root system. Believing would not only remove it but also cause it to be replanted in the sea.

Was this a lesson in agriculture? Was Jesus teaching his disciples how they could get rid of literal trees? Not at all. Jesus was explaining to them about faith, and he used an example of something that was impossible. He was teaching them that with faith, or believing, one can do the impossible.

This was not the only time he taught them they could do the impossible. On another occasion, after they were a bit astonished about a certain fig tree Jesus cursed, he told them to "have faith in God," or believe God. He then went on to tell them if they believed and did not doubt, they could say to a mountain, "Be thou removed, and be thou cast into the sea; it shall be done," (Matthew 21:19-21).

Of course, Jesus was certainly not telling them anytime they fancied uprooting a sycamine tree or rearranging a mountain range they could simply believe it and do it; that is absurd. He was teaching them about faith or believing.

He gave two examples of doing the impossible by faith or believing. There are two things Jesus said they could remove by believing and speaking to them directly: a sycamine tree with its enormous root system and a mountain. He was clear that it was not the amount of faith or believing they had, but that they had it. The context of both was faith, or believing God.

If God gives someone revelation to remove a literal sycamine tree, or any tree for that matter, and that person believes Him, he or she can indeed remove the tree and send it into the sea. The same is true for a literal mountain. The point is, it is true for anything impossible that God reveals.

Jesus taught them about believing God to do the impossible: plucking up a sycamine tree by the roots and replanting it in the sea and removing a mountain and casting it into the sea. In this record, understanding the mustard seed and the sycamine tree helps us to see how emphatically he answered their inquiry about faith and how with faith the impossible comes to pass.

Luke 17:5 and 6
And the apostles said unto the Lord, increase our faith.

And the Lord said, If ye had faith as a grain of mustard seed, ye might say unto this sycamine tree, be thou plucked up by the root, and be thou planted in the sea; and it should obey you.

Mark 11:22 and 23
And Jesus answering saith unto them, Have faith in God.

For verily I say unto you, That whosoever shall say unto this mountain, Be thou removed, and be thou cast into the sea; and shall not doubt in his heart, but shall believe that those things which he saith shall come to pass; he shall have whatsoever he saith.

Luke 13:19
It is like a grain of mustard seed, which a man took, and cast into his garden; and it grew, and waxed a great tree; and the fowls of the air lodged in the branches of it.

Chapter 34

Beware of the Leaven

Then Jesus said unto them, Take heed and beware of
the leaven of the Pharisees and of the Sadducees. Matthew 16:6

There was an occasion when Jesus told his followers, "Beware of the leaven of the Pharisees and of the Sadducees." On another occasion, he compared the kingdom of God to leaven. Understanding the leaven of biblical times gives great insight into what he was teaching them.

When reading the word "leaven" in the Bible, many people think of the properties of yeast, that which causes dough to rise. However, that is not the purpose of the leaven used in biblical times. In fact, as we have already discussed, their bread was flat, and as such, causing the dough to rise was not a concern.

Leaven was very thin dough made from flour and water; it was a soupy substance. It was "fermented dough reserved for producing fermentation in a new batch of dough."[25] They would take this thin dough and put it into a two or three-gallon pot and tie off the top with a piece of linen.

For eleven days they put the pot outside in the sun from 6a.m. to 6p.m. After the eleven days, the pot was brought back into the kitchen. Whenever they would bake bread, they added two or three spoonful of this leaven to the dough to sweeten it. The spoonful would permeate all the dough it was added into. Their prepared bread was no longer just pure dough.

What is important to recognize in the implied comparison Jesus was making is that leaven literally permeates and changes the dough. In our modern dictionary, there are several definitions for the word "leaven." Most people think leaven and yeast are the same thing. However, one of the definitions says, "an element that produces an altering or

---

25   Random House Webster's College Dictionary, 2nd Revised and Updated ed., s.v. "leaven."

transforming influence."[26] That definition is very accurate when considering leaven talked about in biblical times.

When Jesus gave his warning about the leaven of the Pharisees as recorded in the gospel of Matthew, his disciples got a bit confused and thought he was talking about literal bread. However, he explained to them that he was talking about the doctrine of the Pharisees and Sadducees.

Jesus compared their doctrine to leaven. They were supposed to be teaching people about God and the things of God, but Jesus was stating they were adding in their own ideas to the pure, right doctrine of God.

Jesus directly confronted the religious leaders of his day many times. On one occasion, he told them their worship was vain and that they were teaching the commandments of men as doctrine. Their message was no longer pure; they had changed it.

Jesus also used the comparison of leaven concerning the kingdom of heaven. The kingdom of heaven, sometimes referred to as the kingdom of God, includes all that God made available through the completed work of Jesus Christ. Because God so loved the world and because of what His Son, Jesus Christ, accomplished, lives of men and women all over the world have been changed.

By accepting Jesus Christ as lord of all men and believing God raised him from the dead, someone lost and without hope can become saved. He or she can be forever changed, born from above, a child of God.

In the book of Galatians, the Apostle Paul told the believers they had been doing well, but then they began thinking they were righteous before God by doing the works of the Law. In other words, they were attempting to make themselves righteous by their good works.

Paul pointed out to them this kind of thinking came in from somewhere else. It had permeated that group of believers. He told them in Galatians 5:9, "A little leaven leavens the whole lump."

In some sectors of Christianity today, things Paul taught and recorded in the epistles have been changed as well. How did that happen?

26   Random House Webster's College Dictionary, 2nd Revised and Updated ed., s.v. "leaven."

Through the years and even unto this day, leaven—ideas, theories, and commandments of men—continues to be added to the pure Word of God. That is why it is of great importance to rightly understand the Scriptures.

Matthew 16:6, 11, 12
Then Jesus said unto them, Take heed and beware of the leaven of the Pharisees and of the Sadducees.

How is it that ye do not understand that I spake it not to you concerning bread, that ye should beware of the leaven of the Pharisees and of the Sadducees?

Then understood they how that he bade them not beware of the leaven of bread, but of the doctrine of the Pharisees and of the Sadducees.

Matthew 15:7-9
Ye hypocrites, well did Esaias prophesy of you, saying,

This people draweth nigh unto me with their mouth, and honoureth me with their lips; but their heart is far from me.

But in vain they do worship me, teaching for doctrines the commandments of men.

Matthew 13:33
Another parable spake he unto them; The kingdom of heaven is like unto leaven, which a woman took, and hid in three measures of meal, till the whole was leavened.

Ephesians 2:5, 8 and 9
Even when we were dead in sins, hath quickened us together with Christ, (by grace ye are saved;)

For by grace are ye saved through faith; and that not of yourselves: it is the gift of God:

Not of works, lest any man should boast.

Romans 10:9
That if thou shalt confess with thy mouth the Lord Jesus, and shalt believe in thine heart that God hath raised him from the dead, thou shalt be saved.

Galatians 5:6-9
For in Jesus Christ neither circumcision availeth any thing, nor uncircumcision; but faith which worketh by love.

Ye did run well; who did hinder you that ye should not obey the truth?

This persuasion cometh not of him that calleth you.

A little leaven leaveneth the whole lump.

Chapter 35

Thou Fool

But I say unto you, That whosoever is angry with his brother without a cause shall be in danger of the judgment: and whosoever shall say to his brother, Raca, shall be in danger of the council: but whosoever shall say, Thou fool, shall be in danger of hell fire. Matthew 5:22

In our culture, there are things we could say or do to insult someone. One could call another stupid or an idiot. The same was true in biblical times; there were cutting words used to insult someone.

Jesus said to call someone "raca" would put them in danger of the council. "Raca" is an Aramaic word that was used to express contempt and scorn. To say "raca" was comparable to spitting in someone's face. Saying "raca" to a Judean was considered degrading, and it was punishable before the Sanhedrin, the ruling council of the Judeans.[27]

Jesus indicated calling someone a "fool" was even worse. E.W. Bullinger defines "raca" as "a contemptuous interjection expressing the emotion or scorn of a disdainful mind." And he defines "fool" as "a wicked reprobate, destitute of all spiritual or Divine knowledge."[28]

In that culture, they believed God was in them. To call someone a fool was not only insulting to the person, but since God was in them, it also meant that God was a wicked reprobate, destitute of all spiritual or Divine knowledge. This was obviously a great insult to God as well.

The Bible describes God's children as being His dwelling place. God's gift of holy spirit is also described by the phrase "Christ in you." As born-again Christians, we may at times disagree or even do things that are unkind or unloving. Perhaps we should think twice about the names or insults we are tempted to voice to one another.

27   Walter J. Cummins, *The Acceptable Year of the Lord* (Scripture Consulting Franklin, Ohio, 2005), 162
28   E.W. Bullinger, *The Companion Bible* (Enlarged type edition, Kregal Publications, Grand Rapids Michigan, 1999),1318_

Jesus said to his followers, "By this shall all men know that you are my disciples, if you have love one to another." Similarly, we have been instructed in I John 3:23, "And this is his commandment, That we should believe on the name of his Son Jesus Christ, and love one another, as he gave us commandment."

Matthew 5:22
But I say unto you, That whosoever is angry with his brother without a cause shall be in danger of the judgment: and whosoever shall say to his brother, Raca, shall be in danger of the council: but whosoever shall say, Thou fool, shall be in danger of hell fire.

I John 4:13
Hereby know we that we dwell in him, and He in us, because He hath given us of His Spirit.

Romans 8:9
But ye are not in the flesh, but in the Spirit, if so be that the Spirit of God dwell in you. Now if any man have not the Spirit of Christ, he is none of his.

II Corinthians 6:16
And what agreement hath the temple of God with idols? for ye are the temple of the living God; as God hath said, I will dwell in them, and walk in them; and I will be their God, and they shall be My people.

Philippians 2:13
For it is God which worketh in you both to will and to do of his good pleasure.

Colossians 1:27
To whom God would make known what is the riches of the glory of this mystery among the Gentiles; which is Christ in you, the hope of glory:

John 13:35
By this shall all men know that ye are my disciples, if ye have love one to another.

I John 3:23
And this is his commandment, That we should believe on the name of his Son Jesus Christ, and love one another, as he gave us commandment.

Chapter 36

Enter into Thy Closet

And when thou prayest, thou shalt not be as the hypocrites are: for they love to pray standing in the synagogues and in the corners of the streets, that they may be seen of men. Verily I say unto you, They have their reward.

But thou, when thou prayest, enter into thy closet, and when thou hast shut thy door, pray to thy Father which is in secret; and thy Father which seeth in secret shall reward thee openly. Mathew 6:5, 6

There is an abundance of verses in the Bible relating to the topic of prayer. Jesus spoke of it often. In the record above, Jesus talked about praying in one's closet.

When he spoke about going into a closet, he was not referring to a literal closet; rather, he was making a very important point about a person's prayer life. Right before suggesting going into the closet, Jesus had explained how not to pray.

He told them not to be like the religious hypocrites of the day who loved to have everyone see them pray. Those who prayed that way wanted people to see just how "spiritual" they were. Jesus said that was their reward.

Instead, he told his followers to go into their closet, shut the door, and then pray. The closet is the closet of the mind where one can be quiet— and not just physically quiet, but more importantly, mentally quiet.

Shutting the door refers to getting rid of or shutting out foreign thoughts, negative thoughts, worrying thoughts, and wandering thoughts. In getting rid of those thoughts, each person can then keep his or her mind stayed upon God. One can talk with Him and listen for His still, small voice.

There are times when it may be difficult to simply shut this figurative door. Perhaps in times of stress, anxiety, worry, or fear it is harder to close the door to get quiet and hear from God. I Peter 5:8 says, "Casting all your care upon him; for he careth for you." When we go into the closet and shut the door, we really can cast all our cares upon Him, because He does indeed care for us.

There are two different Greek words translated "care" in that verse. The first use, "casting all your care," means anxious cares, or troubles. The second use, "he careth for you," means the object of care or interest.[29] In other words, we can give God all our troubles, anxieties, and stress because He cares for us; we are the object of his care and He will provide what we need.

Isn't that a really a beautiful and powerful verse regarding prayer? We cast, or give, all our anxiety, worry, and fears to God and He will take care of us, give us what is needed and provide a solution.

Instead of praying like the hypocrites who just loved for people to see them praying, Jesus talked about going into our closet, getting quiet with God so we can cast all of our cares to God.

Mathew 6:5 - 7
And when thou prayest, thou shalt not be as the hypocrites are: for they love to pray standing in the synagogues and in the corners of the streets, that they may be seen of men. Verily I say unto you, They have their reward.

But thou, when thou prayest, enter into thy closet, and when thou hast shut thy door, pray to thy Father which is in secret; and thy Father which seeth in secret shall reward thee openly.

But when ye pray, use not vain repetitions, as the heathen do: for they think that they shall be heard for their much speaking.

I Peter 5:7
Casting all your care upon him; for he careth for you.

---

29   E.W. Bullinger, *A Critical Lexicon and Concordance to the English and Greek New Testament* (Zondervan Printing 1975), *134*

Chapter 37

A Fig Tree

And seeing a fig tree afar off having leaves, he came, if haply he might find any thing thereon: and when he came to it, he found nothing but leaves; for the time of figs was not yet.

And Jesus answered and said unto it, No man eat fruit of thee hereafter for ever. And his disciples heard it. Mark 11:13,14

This is an incident in the Gospel of Mark where Jesus saw a fig tree and walked over to it hoping to find something to eat. The record says he found nothing but leaves. It was not the time or season for figs. Then Jesus cursed the tree by saying, "No man eat fruit of thee hereafter forever."

One might wonder why Jesus would go over to a tree when it was not the season for fruit. It would seem foolish to approach a fruit tree out of its season, but once again, knowing about the culture of those alive during this biblical time period provides understanding.

This type of fig tree is often referred to as "the people's tree," meaning anyone can help themselves to the fruit. The figs on the tree mature in June. However, in early spring, there are little buds on the tree that later turn into mature figs. These buds are very sweet and make for a nice snack.

Jesus was not ignorant of the fruit trees in his land, nor was he confused by what season it was. He simply approached the tree for something to eat. However, this tree had no buds. Having no buds in the springtime meant it would not have fruit later.

This tree had become a fruitless, barren tree. His cursing of the tree was not in disappointment of not finding any sweet buds. Rather, his statement was true of that tree, but there is a deeper meaning as well.

The nation of Israel, God's chosen people, is represented figuratively by the fig tree several times in the Old Testament. It is noteworthy this incident recorded in the Gospel of Mark occurred shortly before the arrest and execution of Jesus Christ.

God sent His son to Israel and they rejected him. Jesus cursing this fig tree was a declaration against Israel. They had rejected their Messiah, the Son of God. Israel had become spiritually fruitless and barren.

Not long after this, Jesus Christ completed mankind's redemption and salvation. As a result, the nation of Israel was no longer God's only people. God threw the doors wide open. Now, because of the completed work of Christ, the Bible declares it makes no difference if one is a Jew or a Gentile, bond or free, male or female. The invitation is to every person on earth. All those who confess Jesus as lord and believe God raised him from the dead are saved.

Mark 11:13 and 14
And seeing a fig tree afar off having leaves, he came, if haply he might find any thing thereon: and when he came to it, he found nothing but leaves; for the time of figs was not yet.

And Jesus answered and said unto it, No man eat fruit of thee hereafter for ever. And his disciples heard it.

John 3:16
For God so loved the world, that he gave his only begotten Son, that whosoever believeth in him should not perish, but have everlasting life.

Galatians 3:28
There is neither Jew nor Greek, there is neither bond nor free, there is neither male nor female: for ye are all one in Christ Jesus.

Romans 10:9
That if thou shalt confess with thy mouth the Lord Jesus, and shalt believe in thine heart that God hath raised him from the dead, thou shalt be saved.

Chapter 38

Pluck Them Out of My Hand

And I give unto them eternal life; and they shall never perish, neither shall any man pluck them out of my hand.

My Father, which gave them me, is greater than all; and no man is able to pluck them out of my Father's hand. John 10:28, 29

While it is very helpful to understand the culture of biblical times, that certainly does not mean we need to adapt or take on their culture. Rather, understanding their culture gives us great insight into the meaning of the Scriptures.

In the Gospel of John, in teaching about eternal life, Jesus Christ said those having eternal life would never perish, and no one would be able to pluck them out of his hand or His Father's hand.

To "pluck out of the hand" refers to a game the young children played in the lands and times of the Bible. This is something those listening to Jesus teach would have readily understood; it painted a clear picture for them. Once we understand the game the children played, we too will have a clear picture of what he said.

Here is the simple game the children played: One of the youngsters would put a coin in his hand, close his fist, and then keep it closed as tightly as he could. Another child would then try to open the tightly clenched fist, and if he could, he would get the coin.

In referring to eternal life, Jesus was saying that no one was going to open his or his Father's fist. In other words, eternal life cannot be taken or altered. This gives a little added insight to a verse in Colossians that says our life is hid with Christ in God—eternal life.

It is very noteworthy when Jesus spoke of eternal life he used the word "perish." He didn't say those who have eternal life would not die, but rather, they would not perish. There is a big difference.

The Greek word translated "perish" in John 10 means to be destroyed and obliterated.[30] While a born-again believer might die, the person will never perish because he or she has eternal life. The Bible says that those who are born again and die are asleep, and they will be made alive when Christ returns. That would not be possible if one were to be destroyed and obliterated.

Because of God's great love, He has freely extended the invitation to all people to accept His son, to believe that Jesus is the savior and lord of all men and that God raised him from the dead. By accepting those truths, one becomes saved and receives eternal life.

Once someone receives eternal life, nothing can take it away. No one can ever be plucked out of Christ's hand, or out of his Father's hand. You will not perish!

Once again, with a little understanding of the times and culture in which the Scriptures were written, the Bible becomes clear and its richness shines brightly.

John 10:28, 29
And I give unto them eternal life; and they shall never perish, neither shall any man pluck them out of my hand.

My Father, which gave them me, is greater than all; and no man is able to pluck them out of my Father's hand.

Colossians 3:3b
Your life is hid with Christ in God

John 3:16
For God so loved the world, that he gave his only begotten Son, that whosoever believeth in him should not perish, but have everlasting life.

Romans 10:9
That if thou shalt confess with thy mouth the Lord Jesus, and shalt

30   E.W. Bullinger, *A Critical Lexicon and Concordance to the English and Greek New Testament* (Zondervan Printing 1975), 581

believe in thine heart that God hath raised him from the dead, thou shalt be saved.

I Thessalonians 4:15-17
For this we say unto you by the word of the Lord, that we which are alive and remain unto the coming of the Lord shall not prevent them which are asleep.

For the Lord himself shall descend from heaven with a shout, with the voice of the archangel, and with the trump of God: and the dead in Christ shall rise first:

Then we which are alive and remain shall be caught up together with them in the clouds, to meet the Lord in the air: and so shall we ever be with the Lord.

Chapter 39

You Are the Salt of the Earth

Ye are the salt of the earth: but if the salt have lost his savour,
wherewith shall it be salted? it is thenceforth good for nothing,
but to be cast out, and to be trodden under foot of men.

Ye are the light of the world. A city that is set on an hill
cannot be hid. Matthew 5:13 and 14

Jesus taught his disciples many things on the occasion referred to as "the sermon on the mount" recorded in Matthew 5. At one point, he compared his disciples to both salt and light. He told them they were the salt of the earth and the light of the world. He elaborated on both of those comparisons.

The phrase "salt of the earth" is still used today. This phrase is used as a compliment, and rightly so. Understanding biblical culture helps us understand the phrase and why it is a compliment.

Salt is a necessity of life. The Bible contains numerous references to salt. In various contexts it is often used metaphorically to signify permanence, loyalty, value, and purification.

Jesus compared the disciples to salt, but he also pointed out that salt can lose its savor, in which case it would not be good for anything. So how does salt lose its savor?

In biblical times, salt was kept in large earthen jars. In *The Acceptable Year of the Lord*, Rev. Cummins states, "Water on the floor would frequently seep into the bottom of the jar and moisten the salt causing it to lose its saltiness. In the course of using the salt, a person would reach the bottom of the jar where this had happened, and he would throw out the watered-down salt into the street where it would be trodden under foot."[31]

31   Walter J. Cummins, *The Acceptable Year of the Lord* (Scripture Consulting Franklin, Ohio, 2005), *160*

When Jesus told his disciples they were the salt of the earth, he also warned them that they could lose their salty savor. In other words, the great qualities of salt like loyalty, durability, and permanence were qualities that one must continue to work to maintain.

He also told them they were the light of the world, but he reminded them they needed to let their light shine and not hide it. In biblical times, artificial light came from oil lamps. These oil lamps were often in a house on small lamp stands, thus giving light to all in the room.

In comparing the disciples to the "light of the world," he instructed them to not hide their light. They were to let their light shine so that others could see their good works and glorify the Father.

We too can let our light shine. We can let people see the light of the truth of God's Word. We can let them see what God is doing in our lives so that our heavenly Father gets the glory.

We can also keep our savor. We can choose to not compromise on our character and the qualities of life that really matter. Without those great qualities in our lives, we would lose our savor and our effectiveness in bringing a message of deliverance to a world that desperately needs it.

Matthew 5:13-16
Ye are the salt of the earth: but if the salt have lost his savour, wherewith shall it be salted? it is thenceforth good for nothing, but to be cast out, and to be trodden under foot of men.

Ye are the light of the world. A city that is set on an hill cannot be hid.

Neither do men light a candle, and put it under a bushel, but on a candlestick; and it giveth light unto all that are in the house.

Let your light so shine before men, that they may see your good works, and glorify your Father which is in heaven.

Chapter 40

Shake Off the Dust of Your Feet

And whosoever shall not receive you, nor hear your words,
when ye depart out of that house or city, shake off the dust of
your feet. Matthew 10:14

In the Gospel of Matthew, Jesus was sending out the twelve to preach. One of the things he told them was if people did not want to hear what they had to say, they were to depart and shake off the dust of their feet.

Paul and Barnabas in Acts 13 "shook off the dust of their feet" when they were expelled out of Antioch. To the western mind that sounds a little odd. In fact, it almost sounds arrogant. However, this statement is not literal. They did not physically take off their sandals and shake the dust off. It is an eastern idiom. It pertains to what one walks away with in his or her mind, what is carried in the mind.

This eastern idiom means to shake off any animosity or bitter feelings felt toward someone. In doing so, one has peace in his or her heart and mind. In other words, do not carry any anger, hurt, blame, resentment, or regret upon leaving someone.

We are encouraged to preach the word of God, and we certainly want people to respond favorably to it. If they do not, however, one might be tempted to be upset with them. Shaking the dust off means do not carry any of that in the mind or heart. The same is true if one is treated poorly. Do not carry any of that either. It is much better to leave it all there and move forward with God's peace in one's heart and mind.

About this topic, Bishop Pillai said, "Dust is symbolic of hatred, malice, grudge, resentment and ill will. Don't carry these things with you, but rather carry only love, no matter how much harm is done unto you."[32]

---

32   Bishop K.C. Pillai, "Matthew" retrieved from http://www.kcpillai.org/bishop-kc-pillai/old-and-new-testament-orientalisms/matthew

Some Christians feel obligated to make people accept and believe the Gospel. However, it is the responsibility of those who hear the message to decide what they will do with it—accept it or reject it. When one shares the Gospel, he or she is simply a messenger like the twelve were, like Paul and Barnabas were.

An individual is not responsible for another's response. When that response is less than favorable, one can shake the dust off his or her feet and move on.

———————

Matthew 10:14:
And whosoever shall not receive you, nor hear your words, when ye depart out of that house or city, shake off the dust of your feet.

Mark 6:11:
And whosoever shall not receive you, nor hear you, when ye depart thence, shake off the dust under your feet for a testimony against them.

Acts 13:51
But they shook off the dust of their feet against them, and came unto Iconium.

Chapter 41

He Washed Their Feet

After that he poureth water into a basin, and began to wash the disciples' feet, and to wipe them with the towel wherewith he was girded. John 13:5

Nowadays, it would be very strange to walk into your friend's house and have them offer to wash your feet. That is not a common practice in our day and time. However, a lot of people are familiar with a foot washing incident that occurred during what is commonly called "The Last Supper." This event took place shortly before Jesus was arrested. While some understand the lesson regarding service, many fail to see an even deeper meaning.

In the lands and times of the Bible, people wore sandals and walked on dusty roads. It was, therefore, very common to have one's feet washed upon entering a friend's house.

The servant who performed this lowly task was usually the lowest servant in the household. However, an exception was if the guest was someone of great importance, someone with a very high rank in society. On those occasions, it was the master of the house who washed the feet.

The master washing a guest's feet was his way of recognizing that person as very important. It was an extremely high compliment.

When Jesus washed the feet of his disciples that night, he was not only teaching them humility and service, but he was also teaching them a great lesson about love. They were well aware their own social status did not deserve that kind of treatment. That is why Peter objected and refused to have Jesus wash his feet.

The love Jesus Christ demonstrated in this situation is astounding. Shortly before he was to suffer and die for the whole world, he treated his disciples like they were royalty. After this meal, he was arrested, beaten, tortured, crucified, and finally, he laid down his life for all of mankind – the greatest act of love anyone has ever done!

Today, we may not have foot washing in our culture, but we can certainly remember this great lesson about love. Jesus told them that night, "By this shall all men know that ye are my disciples, if ye have love one to another." May we walk with that same love.

John 13:4-17

He riseth from supper, and laid aside his garments; and took a towel, and girded himself.

After that he poureth water into a basin, and began to wash the disciples' feet, and to wipe them with the towel wherewith he was girded.

Then cometh he to Simon Peter: and Peter saith unto him, Lord, dost thou wash my feet?

Jesus answered and said unto him, What I do thou knowest not now; but thou shalt know hereafter.

Peter saith unto him, Thou shalt never wash my feet. Jesus answered him, If I wash thee not, thou hast no part with me.

Simon Peter saith unto him, Lord, not my feet only, but also my hands and my head.

Jesus saith to him, He that is washed needeth not save to wash his feet, but is clean every whit: and ye are clean, but not all.

For he knew who should betray him; therefore said he, Ye are not all clean.

So after he had washed their feet, and had taken his garments, and was set down again, he said unto them, Know ye what I have done to you?

Ye call me Master and Lord: and ye say well; for so I am.

If I then, your Lord and Master, have washed your feet; ye also ought to wash one another's feet.

For I have given you an example, that ye should do as I have done to you.

Verily, verily, I say unto you, The servant is not greater than his lord; neither he that is sent greater than he that sent him.

If ye know these things, happy are ye if ye do them.

John 15:13
Greater love hath no man than this, that a man lay down his life for his friends.

John 13:35
By this shall all men know that ye are my disciples, if ye have love one to another.

Chapter 42

Jesus Gave Judas the Sop

Jesus answered, He it is, to whom I shall give a sop,
when I have dipped it. And when he had dipped the sop,
he gave it to Judas Iscariot, the son of Simon. John 13:26

The event referred to as "The Last Supper" took place shortly before Jesus was arrested. There were many significant things that happened that evening. One of those was Jesus giving Judas the sop.

By the time of the meal, Judas had already arranged to betray Jesus for thirty pieces of silver. It was a dastardly act to say the least, and according to the record in Mark 14, Jesus already knew who his traitor was by this last meal. Jesus not only knew Judas was going to betray him, but according to Matthew 26, Judas also knew that Jesus knew. Yet, Jesus gave Judas the sop. What is the significance of the sop?

The two most honored seats at a meal were those to the right and left of the host or the master. That means the disciple whom Jesus loved, who rested his head on Jesus' bosom (an act of deep concern, love, and intimate friendship) was sitting at one of the positions of honor at this meal. Likewise, for Jesus to be able to give Judas the sop, Judas would have also had to be near Jesus, quite possibly in the other honored position.

The word "sop" simply means a small portion; "a little bit, a morsel."[33] In our western culture today, we do not use the word "sop." We use phrases like, a dab, a little piece, or a small bite. Sop is just a word for a small piece of food.

In biblical times, it would have been customary to have a common dish on the table that everyone shared. The flat, thin bread they ate was often used to dip into the common dish and wrap it around a small piece of food, a sop.

33   E.W. Bullinger, *A Critical Lexicon and Concordance to the English and Greek New Testament* (Zondervan Printing 1975), 718

The host or master of the house gave the sop to the person to whom he wanted to show his greatest love and esteem. He did that by dipping into the common dish and then placing the sop in the person's mouth. This showed to all those present, and especially to the person receiving the sop, the love and honor he had for him.

Picturing this scene gives me chills. Jesus knew Judas was about to betray him. Judas knew Jesus knew. Yet, Jesus gave him the sop. By extending so much honor and love to Judas, Jesus gave him a chance to change his plans. The incredible and unconditional love Jesus demonstrated here is truly amazing.

God gives everyone free will to choose their own paths. For Judas, however, even an act of love and honor directly from the Lord Jesus Christ himself did not guarantee he would do the right thing—how sad for Judas.

John 13:21 - 30

When Jesus had thus said, he was troubled in spirit, and testified, and said, Verily, verily, I say unto you, that one of you shall betray me.

Then the disciples looked one on another, doubting of whom he spake.

Now there was leaning on Jesus' bosom one of his disciples, whom Jesus loved.

Simon Peter therefore beckoned to him, that he should ask who it should be of whom he spake.

He then lying on Jesus' breast saith unto him, Lord, who is it?

Jesus answered, He it is, to whom I shall give a sop, when I have dipped it. And when he had dipped the sop, he gave it to Judas Iscariot, the son of Simon.

And after the sop Satan entered into him. Then said Jesus unto him, That thou doest, do quickly.

Now no man at the table knew for what intent he spake this unto him.

For some of them thought, because Judas had the bag, that Jesus had said unto him, Buy those things that we have need of against the feast; or, that he should give something to the poor.

He then having received the sop went immediately out: and it was night.

Mark 14:18-20:
And as they sat and did eat, Jesus said, Verily I say unto you, One of you which eateth with me shall betray me.

And they began to be sorrowful, and to say unto him one by one, Is it I? and another said, Is it I?

And he answered and said unto them, It is one of the twelve, that dippeth with me in the dish.

Matthew 26:25
Then Judas, which betrayed him, answered and said, Master, is it I? He said unto him, Thou hast said.

Chapter 43

Coals of Fire on His Head

Therefore if thine enemy hunger, feed him;
if he thirst, give him drink: for in so doing thou shalt
heap coals of fire on his head. Romans 12:20

This verse in the book of Romans talks about doing some things for one's enemy that will "heap coals of fire on his head." Some think this is referring to some sort of revenge. However, it means nothing of the sort. Understanding the culture in biblical times unlocks this simple, yet powerful verse.

It was common practice back then for a young boy in the village to take hot coals from the first fire of the morning and put them into a piece of pottery. The boy would then carry the pottery with the hot coals inside balanced upon his head to the other households in the village. Arriving at the first household, they would take a hot coal to start their own fire. He would then go to the next family so they could get a coal to start their fire, and so on.

Doing this task on cold mornings would actually be pleasant. The heat from the coals in the pottery would warm the young boy. As he went from family to family, he stayed nice and warm performing this simple duty.

The things Romans 12 talks about doing for one's enemy that results in heaping coals of fire on his head has nothing to do with revenge or retaliation. Rather, in doing those things one might warm his or her heart, and they just might change in the process.

One may never know how a smile, a kind word, or a loving action can impact someone else's life. As God's children, we endeavor to exhibit our Father's love to everyone we meet. The Bible instructs us that if possible, live peaceably with all people.

Romans 12:17-21
Recompense to no man evil for evil. Provide things honest in the sight of all men.

If it be possible, as much as lieth in you, live peaceably with all men.

Dearly beloved, avenge not yourselves, but rather give place unto wrath: for it is written, Vengeance is mine; I will repay, saith the Lord.

Therefore if thine enemy hunger, feed him; if he thirst, give him drink: for in so doing thou shalt heap coals of fire on his head.

Be not overcome of evil, but overcome evil with good.

Chapter 44

Laid It at the Apostles' Feet

Having land, sold it, and brought the money,
and laid it at the apostles' feet. Acts 4:37

In the lands and times of the Bible, when a man of God was leaving a home after visiting, he would pray with the people and bless their home. The people of that house would then hand him a tray that contained fruits and flowers. He could pick what he wanted from the tray before leaving the house.

However, if they were giving him money, they did not put it on the tray. Instead, it would be wrapped and placed at his feet. They did this to indicate money was only a servant; money was not their God.

There is nothing evil about money. Money is not the root of all evil; the Bible says in I Timothy 6:10, "for the love of money is the root of all evil..." We need and utilize money to carry out the daily affairs of life.

There are numerous wonderful believers recorded in the Bible who had great wealth, but their love and trust was in God, not their wealth. Problems arise when a person begins to love money. When that happens, money ceases to be a necessary servant.

In the United States, printed or stamped on all our money we read the words: "In God We Trust." What a wonderful reminder every time we use money that we should trust in our God and not in our money.

Acts 4:37
Having land, sold it, and brought the money, and laid it at the apostles' feet.

Acts 4:35
And laid them down at the apostles' feet: and distribution was made unto every man according as he had need.

Acts 5:2
And kept back part of the price, his wife also being privy to it, and brought a certain part, and laid it at the apostles' feet.

I Timothy 6:10
For the love of money is the root of all evil: which while some coveted after, they have erred from the faith, and pierced themselves through with many sorrows.

Chapter 45

Upon the Housetop

On the morrow, as they went on their journey, and drew nigh unto the city, Peter went up upon the housetop to pray about the sixth hour:
Acts 10:9

In reading the Bible, we must be cautious to not read our modern western culture into the Scriptures. At times, it is easy to read words or phrases that instantly paint a picture in our minds of what we are used to seeing or hearing. However, we must always try to remind ourselves of what the biblical culture looked like.

For example, like most roofs on homes in the United States, mine is pitched. I venture up there on rare occasion for maintenance on the air conditioner. Other than that, I hardly ever go up on my roof. When I read about Peter going up upon the housetop to pray, what picture do I have in my mind?

In the lands and times of the Bible, the roofs were flat. It was common for people to go up on the roof, or the housetop, for various reasons. It was generally a quiet place away from other people. It served as a great place to teach children in the evening or to have a private conversation with someone. It was also very common to go up on the housetop to pray.

Housetops would normally be accessible by a side ladder or stairs from the courtyard and, at times, from the inside where a hatch could open and close.

There is a record in Isaiah indicating something ailing the entire population so extraordinarily that it talks about "wholly going up on the housetops." This kind of situation would generally be a response to something affecting everyone, a sort of national emergency like an approaching plague or even the expectation of the enemy. Everyone would be on their housetop praying to God and asking for His deliverance from the impending calamity.

So, the next time you are reading the Bible and you see the word "housetop," remember, their roofs were different than our modern pitched roofs. They were flat, and it was common for them to go up on the housetop, especially to pray.

Acts 10:9
On the morrow, as they went on their journey, and drew nigh unto the city, Peter went up upon the housetop to pray about the sixth hour:

I Samuel 9:25
And when they were come down from the high place into the city, Samuel communed with Saul upon the top of the house.

Isaiah 22:1
The burden of the valley of vision. What aileth thee now, that thou art wholly gone up to the housetops?

Chapter 46

Laid Down Their Clothes at a Young Man's Feet

And cast him out of the city, and stoned him: and the witnesses
laid down their clothes at a young man's feet, whose name
was Saul. Acts 7:58

After a very remarkable presentation by Stephen to his accusers, the record in Acts 7 ends with the religious leaders executing this wonderful man. They stoned him to death. It is indeed a very sad account to read.

There is a part of verse 58 that is often misunderstood. Why would the witnesses lay down their clothes at Saul's feet? What clothes?

These witnesses laid down their clothes, or cloaks at Saul's feet. They were not the ones doing the stoning, but rather, they were witnesses of the execution. In *A Journey through the Acts and Epistles*, Rev. Cummins explains, "This was a custom in the lands and times of the Bible practiced by those who were genuine witnesses of an event or transaction."[34]

We learn in the next Chapter this man named Saul (who is also called Paul) was consenting, or approving, of Stephen's death. He was spearheading the persecution against the followers of Jesus Christ. He ravaged the church entering houses and dragging men and women to prison.

In other Scriptures we learn he had authority to do all of this from the chief priests. He not only put them in prison but also compelled them to blaspheme, and he gave his vote to put many of them to death.

As terrible as his actions were, those familiar with the Bible know Paul had a life changing experience on his way to Damascus in pursuit of persecuting even more followers of Jesus. The very man advancing this murderous persecution converted to Christianity. Who would have ever thought this was possible?

34   Walter J. Cummins, *A Journey through the Acts and Epistles, Volume 1* (Scripture Consulting Franklin, Ohio, 2006), 52

Paul accepted what Christ accomplished for all believers including God's forgiveness. He spent the rest of his life preaching the gospel concerning Jesus Christ, walking with the power of God, and writing much of the New Testament. In several places in those writings, he humbly and gratefully declared what God had done for him.

Have you ever considered that if this man responsible for murdering God's people could change, then change must be available for anyone. Perhaps we would do well not to prejudge or prequalify anyone from accepting Jesus Christ.

Not only that, but also consider how God forgave this man of all the terrible acts he did. Paul could have lived his life in utter condemnation for what he had done, but instead he chose to accept God's forgiveness. If God could graciously forgive Paul, He can certainly forgive anyone.

Acts 7:58
And cast him out of the city, and stoned him: and the witnesses laid down their clothes at a young man's feet, whose name was Saul.

Acts 8:1-3
And Saul was consenting unto his death. And at that time there was a great persecution against the church which was at Jerusalem; and they were all scattered abroad throughout the regions of Judaea and Samaria, except the apostles.

And devout men carried Stephen to his burial, and made great lamentation over him.

As for Saul, he made havock of the church, entering into every house, and haling men and women committed them to prison.

Acts 9:1 and 2
And Saul, yet breathing out threatenings and slaughter against the disciples of the Lord, went unto the high priest,

And desired of him letters to Damascus to the synagogues, that if he found any of this way, whether they were men or women, he might bring them bound unto Jerusalem.

Acts 22:3-6
I am verily a man which am a Jew, born in Tarsus, a city in Cilicia, yet brought up in this city at the feet of Gamaliel, and taught according to the perfect manner of the law of the fathers, and was zealous toward God, as ye all are this day.

And I persecuted this way unto the death, binding and delivering into prisons both men and women.

As also the high priest doth bear me witness, and all the estate of the elders: from whom also I received letters unto the brethren, and went to Damascus, to bring them which were there bound unto Jerusalem, for to be punished.

And it came to pass, that, as I made my journey, and was come nigh unto Damascus about noon, suddenly there shone from heaven a great light round about me.

Acts 26:9-12
I verily thought with myself, that I ought to do many things contrary to the name of Jesus of Nazareth.

Which thing I also did in Jerusalem: and many of the saints did I shut up in prison, having received authority from the chief priests; and when they were put to death, I gave my voice against them.

And I punished them oft in every synagogue, and compelled them to blaspheme; and being exceedingly mad against them, I persecuted them even unto strange cities.

Whereupon as I went to Damascus with authority and commission from the chief priests,

Galatians 1:13
For ye have heard of my conversation in time past in the Jews' religion, how that beyond measure I persecuted the church of God, and wasted it:

Acts 9:1-30
And Saul, yet breathing out threatenings and slaughter against the disciples of the Lord, went unto the high priest,

And desired of him letters to Damascus to the synagogues, that if he found any of this way, whether they were men or women, he might bring them bound unto Jerusalem.

And as he journeyed, he came near Damascus: and suddenly there shined round about him a light from heaven:

And he fell to the earth, and heard a voice saying unto him, Saul, Saul, why persecutest thou me?

And he said, Who art thou, Lord? And the Lord said, I am Jesus whom thou persecutest: it is hard for thee to kick against the pricks.

And he trembling and astonished said, Lord, what wilt thou have me to do? And the Lord said unto him, Arise, and go into the city, and it shall be told thee what thou must do.

And the men which journeyed with him stood speechless, hearing a voice, but seeing no man.

And Saul arose from the earth; and when his eyes were opened, he saw no man: but they led him by the hand, and brought him into Damascus.

And he was three days without sight, and neither did eat nor drink.

And there was a certain disciple at Damascus, named Ananias; and to him said the Lord in a vision, Ananias. And he said, Behold, I am here, Lord.

And the Lord said unto him, Arise, and go into the street which is called Straight, and enquire in the house of Judas for one called Saul, of Tarsus: for, behold, he prayeth,

And hath seen in a vision a man named Ananias coming in, and putting his hand on him, that he might receive his sight.

Then Ananias answered, Lord, I have heard by many of this man, how much evil he hath done to thy saints at Jerusalem:

And here he hath authority from the chief priests to bind all that call on thy name.

But the Lord said unto him, Go thy way: for he is a chosen vessel unto me, to bear my name before the Gentiles, and kings, and the children of Israel:

For I will shew him how great things he must suffer for my name's sake.

And Ananias went his way, and entered into the house; and putting his hands on him said, Brother Saul, the Lord, even Jesus, that appeared unto thee in the way as thou camest, hath sent me, that thou mightest receive thy sight, and be filled with the Holy Ghost.

And immediately there fell from his eyes as it had been scales: and he received sight forthwith, and arose, and was baptized.

And when he had received meat, he was strengthened. Then was Saul certain days with the disciples which were at Damascus.

And straightway he preached Christ in the synagogues, that he is the Son of God.

But all that heard him were amazed, and said; Is not this he that destroyed them which called on this name in Jerusalem, and came hither for that intent, that he might bring them bound unto the chief priests?

But Saul increased the more in strength, and confounded the Jews which dwelt at Damascus, proving that this is very Christ.

And after that many days were fulfilled, the Jews took counsel to kill him:

But their laying await was known of Saul. And they watched the gates day and night to kill him.

Then the disciples took him by night, and let him down by the wall in a basket.

And when Saul was come to Jerusalem, he assayed to join himself to the disciples: but they were all afraid of him, and believed not that he was a disciple.

But Barnabas took him, and brought him to the apostles, and declared unto them how he had seen the Lord in the way, and that he had spoken to him, and how he had preached boldly at Damascus in the name of Jesus.

And he was with them coming in and going out at Jerusalem.

And he spake boldly in the name of the Lord Jesus, and disputed against the Grecians: but they went about to slay him.

Which when the brethren knew, they brought him down to Caesarea, and sent him forth to Tarsus.

I Corinthians 15: 9 and 10
For I am the least of the apostles, that am not meet to be called an apostle, because I persecuted the church of God.

But by the grace of God I am what I am: and his grace which was bestowed upon me was not in vain; but I laboured more abundantly than they all: yet not I, but the grace of God which was with me.

II Timothy 4:7
I have fought a good fight, I have finished my course, I have kept the faith:

Chapter 47

A Thorn in the Flesh

*And lest I should be exalted above measure through the abundance
of the revelations, there was given to me a thorn in the flesh,
the messenger of Satan to buffet me, lest I should be exalted above
measure. II Corinthians 12:7*

As discussed previously, an idiom is a combination of words with a figurative meaning peculiar to a people, community, or class. An idiom's figurative meaning is separate from the literal meaning. Every language and culture has its own idioms.

For example, in western culture if someone is not speaking the truth, one might say, "You're pulling my leg." One who paid a lot of money for something could say, "This item cost me an arm and a leg." Those statements are not literally true, they are idioms.

One of the simplest, yet often misunderstood idioms in the Bible is in II Corinthians 12, commonly referred to as Paul's "thorn in the flesh." Paul states very clearly in the verse he was given "a thorn in the flesh, the messenger of Satan." Therefore, by his own words, his thorn in the flesh was the messenger of, or from, Satan.

In the Old Testament, idioms like the one here in II Corinthians are used to describe people or nations that would potentially be harmful to God's people. They are stated as "pricks in your eyes, thorns in your sides, scourges in your sides, and thorns in your eyes." Clearly, those references were about people.

By reading the book of Acts and the Church Epistles, it is obvious to see how badly Paul was treated by people, especially religious people. Today, one might say those people were "a pain in the butt" or "a pain in the neck." One of the idioms from Paul's culture referring to bothersome people was, "a thorn in the flesh."

It is clear in the verse where this thorn in the flesh came from. It was a messenger of Satan. Satan sent the thorn in the flesh. The purpose of Paul's thorn in the flesh, the messenger of Satan, was to buffet Paul. Satan was trying to stop Paul from preaching the Gospel. Agents of Satan brought the beatings, imprisonments, shipwrecks, and false brethren.

Paul prayed and asked God three times to get rid of his thorn in the flesh. God's answer to him was that His grace was sufficient for Paul. He faced and endured many hardships, and yet, God provided deliverance time and again.

Until God sends His Son back, there is evil in this world; there will be persecutions from Satan. However, there is always God's grace to help in time of need. His grace is sufficient. Pray and ask Him for His deliverance.

II Corinthians 12:7-10
And lest I should be exalted above measure through the abundance of the revelations, there was given to me a thorn in the flesh, the messenger of Satan to buffet me, lest I should be exalted above measure.

For this thing I besought the Lord thrice, that it might depart from me.

And he said unto me, My grace is sufficient for thee: for my strength is made perfect in weakness. Most gladly therefore will I rather glory in my infirmities, that the power of Christ may rest upon me.

Therefore I take pleasure in infirmities, in reproaches, in necessities, in persecutions, in distresses for Christ's sake: for when I am weak, then am I strong.

Numbers 33:55
But if ye will not drive out the inhabitants of the land from before you; then it shall come to pass, that those which ye let remain of them shall be pricks in your eyes, and thorns in your sides, and shall vex you in the land wherein ye dwell.

II Corinthians 11:24-27
Of the Jews five times received I forty stripes save one.

Thrice was I beaten with rods, once was I stoned, thrice I suffered shipwreck, a night and a day I have been in the deep;

in journeyings often, in perils of waters, in perils of robbers, in perils by mine own countrymen, in perils by the heathen, in perils in the city, in perils in the wilderness, in perils in the sea, in perils among false brethren;

in weariness and painfulness, in watchings often, in hunger and thirst, in fastings often, in cold and nakedness.

II Timothy 3:11
Persecutions, afflictions, which came unto me at Antioch, at Iconium, at Lystra; what persecutions I endured: but out of them all the Lord delivered me.

II Corinthians 1:9 and 10
But we had the sentence of death in ourselves, that we should not trust in ourselves, but in God which raiseth the dead:

Who delivered us from so great a death, and doth deliver: in whom we trust that he will yet deliver us;

Chapter 48

A Viper Fastened on His Hand

And when Paul had gathered a bundle of sticks, and laid them on the fire, there came a viper out of the heat, and fastened on his hand.
Acts 28:3

On his way to Rome, the Apostle Paul was shipwrecked and ended up on the island of present day Malta, which is referred to as Melita in the book of Acts. Miraculously, after enduring a tremendous storm for many days, everyone on the ship made it to shore safely.

On that cold, rainy night, Paul and others were gathered around a fire to warm themselves. The barbarous people of the island kindled the fire. The word "barbarous" in this record in Acts simply means they spoke a different language.

The record goes on to say Paul gathered a bundle of sticks for the fire. In the lands and times of the Bible, those warmed by a fire were expected to contribute to the fire. Therefore, Paul contributed by placing a bundle of sticks on it, but as he did, a viper came out of the fire and fastened itself on his hand.

According to Bishop Pillai, the viper that attacked Paul was extremely deadly; it was six to eight inches long with a very pointed head. These vipers could sink their fangs in an inch deep into the skin, and then release their deadly poison. After this type of viper strikes, it dies. It is very difficult to pull the viper's fangs out, even after it is dead.

In biblical times, many believed if a man committed a murder and then ran away to escape the law, a viper would hunt him, find him, and justice would be served. That is why when the people of Malta saw the viper hanging from Paul's hand, they assumed he was a murderer who had escaped justice and was getting what he deserved: death.[35]

---

35   Bishop K.C. Pillai, "Acts" retrieved from http://www.kcpillai.org/bishop-kc-pillai/old-and-new-testament-orientalisms/acts

However, Paul did not die; he operated a power far greater than deadly viper poison—the power of God. The record says he simply shook off the viper into the fire and felt no harm. It was miraculous to shake it off considering how vipers attach to the skin, and it was equally miraculous that he was not harmed by the viper.

The type of viper that bit Paul would typically leave the victim dead within 20 minutes after the strike. There was no cure. Yet, Paul just shook it off, and the people of the island could not believe he did not just fall over dead.

After a short period of time, when Paul showed no signs of any harm, the natives changed their minds and declared Paul was a god. Perhaps that is understandable. They believed their god would send a viper to execute justice, and since the deadly viper had no effect in this case, they concluded this man must be a god.

Paul and those with him were stranded on the island for three months waiting for another ship. Paul ministered to the people on the island during that time, including bringing healing to the father of the chief man on the island. The incident with the viper opened doors for Paul to minister and teach.

Several years ago while briefly visiting the island of Malta, I took a trip to what is called St. Paul's Bay, the area they believe the Apostle Paul and the rest from the ship had landed. It was exciting to be where Paul may have been in what was an awful, life threatening situation.

It is interesting to ponder what happened in Paul's mind in the few seconds from the attack of the viper to shaking it off. The Bible does not say. However, previously on the ship before the wreck, Paul believed the angel's message that all aboard would be saved. They all made it safely to shore, and Paul obviously continued to believe and trust God

We may never end up with a viper hanging from our hand, but we still face our own circumstances and situations, some more serious than others. We can choose to mentally shake off fears and worries and replace them with the promises from God. The God of the Bible is still a powerful and delivering God today.

Acts 28:1-11

And when they were escaped, then they knew that the island was called Melita.

And the barbarous people shewed us no little kindness: for they kindled a fire, and received us every one, because of the present rain, and because of the cold.

And when Paul had gathered a bundle of sticks, and laid them on the fire, there came a viper out of the heat, and fastened on his hand.

And when the barbarians saw the venomous beast hang on his hand, they said among themselves, No doubt this man is a murderer, whom, though he hath escaped the sea, yet vengeance suffereth not to live.

And he shook off the beast into the fire, and felt no harm.

Howbeit they looked when he should have swollen, or fallen down dead suddenly: but after they had looked a great while, and saw no harm come to him, they changed their minds, and said that he was a god.

In the same quarters were possessions of the chief man of the island, whose name was Publius; who received us, and lodged us three days courteously.

And it came to pass, that the father of Publius lay sick of a fever and of a bloody flux: to whom Paul entered in, and prayed, and laid his hands on him, and healed him.

So when this was done, others also, which had diseases in the island, came, and were healed:

Who also honoured us with many honours; and when we departed, they laded us with such things as were necessary.

And after three months we departed in a ship of Alexandria, which had wintered in the isle, whose sign was Castor and Pollux.

Acts 27:20 -26

And when neither sun nor stars in many days appeared, and no small tempest lay on us, all hope that we should be saved was then taken away.

But after long abstinence Paul stood forth in the midst of them, and said, Sirs, ye should have hearkened unto me, and not have loosed from Crete, and to have gained this harm and loss.

And now I exhort you to be of good cheer: for there shall be no loss of any man's life among you, but of the ship.

For there stood by me this night the angel of God, whose I am, and whom I serve,

Saying, Fear not, Paul; thou must be brought before Caesar: and, lo, God hath given thee all them that sail with thee.

Wherefore, sirs, be of good cheer: for I believe God, that it shall be even as it was told me.

Howbeit we must be cast upon a certain island.

Chapter 49

Paul's Girdle

And when he was come unto us, he took Paul's girdle, and bound
his own hands and feet, and said, Thus saith the Holy Ghost,
So shall the Jews at Jerusalem bind the man that owneth this girdle,
and shall deliver him into the hands of the Gentiles. Acts 21:11

There is a very interesting event recorded in Acts 21. The Apostle Paul was on a journey to Jerusalem and stopped to stay in Caesarea at the home of Philip the Evangelist. A prophet from Judea named Agabus came to the house with a message from God for Paul. However, he gave Paul the message in a rather dramatic fashion.

Agabus took Paul's girdle, bound his hands and feet, and then told Paul, "Thus saith the Holy Ghost, So shall the Jews at Jerusalem bind the man that owneth this girdle, and shall deliver him into the hands of the Gentiles."

What was Paul's "girdle"? His girdle was similar to what we might call a belt, sash, or cord. In many cases in biblical times it was hollow so the girdle served not only to secure flowing garments but also carry money.

There are other records in the Bible that show prophets delivering messages in dramatic ways, adding to their words something very visual. Isaiah, Ezekiel, and others used this form of communication to call attention, to give a distinct and impressive idea of the subject, and by engaging the imagination, to fix it in the memory.

Acts 21:8-15
And the next day we that were of Paul's company departed, and came unto Caesarea: and we entered into the house of Philip the evangelist, which was one of the seven; and abode with him.

And the same man had four daughters, virgins, which did prophesy.

And as we tarried there many days, there came down from Judaea a certain prophet, named Agabus.

And when he was come unto us, he took Paul's girdle, and bound his own hands and feet, and said, Thus saith the Holy Ghost, So shall the Jews at Jerusalem bind the man that owneth this girdle, and shall deliver him into the hands of the Gentiles.

And when we heard these things, both we, and they of that place, besought him not to go up to Jerusalem.

Then Paul answered, What mean ye to weep and to break mine heart? for I am ready not to be bound only, but also to die at Jerusalem for the name of the Lord Jesus.

And when he would not be persuaded, we ceased, saying, The will of the Lord be done.

And after those days we took up our carriages, and went up to Jerusalem.

Chapter 50

The Gates of Hell Shall Not Prevail Against It

And I say also unto thee, That thou art Peter, and upon this rock I will build my church; and the gates of hell shall not prevail against it. Matthew 16:18

The only place in the Scriptures the expression, "gates of hell" occurs is in the verse above in Matthew 16 (for full context, see below). That makes it very unique, and the context in which Jesus used that expression is significant.

Jesus asked his disciples who other people were saying he was. Then he asked them, "But who do you say that I am?" Simon Peter answered immediately and said, "You are the Christ, the Son of the living God."

Jesus said, "I will build my church and the gates of hell shall not prevail against it." What does it mean when he said the gates of hell would not prevail against Christ's church? Was he speaking of literal gates, and what exactly is "hell"?

In this verse, the word "hell" is translated from the Greek word "hades." Hades means the grave, or state of death.[36] Contrary to popular opinion, the word "hades" has nothing to do with burning or fire.

Acts 2 talks about Jesus not being left in hades. Jesus died and was buried. Thus, he was in hades, the grave, for three days and three nights, and then God raised him from the dead.

Christ came to bring eternal life, and nothing, not even death or the grave, shall prevail against Christ's church and all he accomplished. Those who have died believing in Christ will not stay in the grave permanently but will be resurrected when Christ returns.

---

36   E.W. Bullinger, *The Companion Bible* (Enlarged type edition, Kregal Publications, Grand Rapids Michigan, 1999), *Appendix 131*

There are no physical gates that lead to death or the grave. The word "gates" is the figure of speech metonymy.[37] According to E.W. Bullinger, "Metonymy is a figure by which one name or noun is used instead of another, to which it stands in a certain relation."[38] Thus, "gates" represents power. Even the power of death or the power of the grave will not prevail against Christ's church.

Christ's church is neither a building nor a denomination. His church is comprised of those who believe in him. Those who are born again are part of the Body of Christ, and Christ is the head of the Body; it is his Church. Nothing, not even the power of death or the grave, will prevail against Christ's church.

The born-again ones, those who confess Jesus as lord and believe in their hearts God has raised him from the dead, are saved. The Bible promises Christ is coming back and will gather together his Body, the Church; we shall meet him in the air, and so shall we ever be with him.

Matthew 16:15-18
He saith unto them, But whom say ye that I am?

And Simon Peter answered and said, Thou art the Christ, the Son of the living God.

And Jesus answered and said unto him, Blessed art thou, Simon Barjona: for flesh and blood hath not revealed it unto thee, but my Father which is in heaven.

And I say also unto thee, That thou art Peter, and upon this rock I will build my church; and the gates of hell shall not prevail against it.

Acts 2:31
He seeing this before spake of the resurrection of Christ, that his soul was not left in hell, neither his flesh did see corruption.

37   E.W. Bullinger, *The Companion Bible* (Enlarged type edition, Kregal Publications, Grand Rapids Michigan, 1999), 1346
38   E.W. Bullinger, *Figures of Speech Used in the Bible* (reprinted 1968 Baker Book House Company), 538

I Corinthians 12:27
Now ye are the body of Christ, and members in particular.

Colossians 1:18
And he is the head of the body, the church: who is the beginning, the firstborn from the dead; that in all things he might have the preeminence.

Romans 10:9
That if thou shalt confess with thy mouth the Lord Jesus, and shalt believe in thine heart that God hath raised him from the dead, thou shalt be saved.

I Thessalonians 4:13-17
But I would not have you to be ignorant, brethren, concerning them which are asleep, that ye sorrow not, even as others which have no hope.

For if we believe that Jesus died and rose again, even so them also which sleep in Jesus will God bring with him.

For this we say unto you by the word of the Lord, that we which are alive and remain unto the coming of the Lord shall not prevent them which are asleep.

For the Lord himself shall descend from heaven with a shout, with the voice of the archangel, and with the trump of God: and the dead in Christ shall rise first:

Then we which are alive and remain shall be caught up together with them in the clouds, to meet the Lord in the air: and so shall we ever be with the Lord.

About the Author

Michael A. Verdicchio spent nearly three decades broadcasting on commercial radio stations all over the U.S., while at the same time promoting gratitude for military veterans both on and off the air. He was both host and co-host of three nationally syndicated radio shows and for over two years wrote, produced, and hosted a weekend radio show, The Optimistic Spin. He has voiced thousands of radio and television commercials.

Michael was ordained to the Christian ministry (non-denomination) in 1982. He is the author of the book, *Healing from God is Available*, as well as several short eBooks including *The Encouraging Word - Getting Older*. He has recorded numerous Christian projects including the 12 CD series, *Stories for Joshua*, the 5 CD set, *Mike's Pep Talks*, as well as *The Seven Church Epistles*, *Healing Words*, *Reducing Stress at Work*, and other projects. His blog of over ten years is called, *Confidence and Joy*.

Michael has shared the Gospel in more than twenty U.S. states and has officiated in numerous weddings and memorial services. He has traveled to nearly a dozen countries. He and his wife of 47 years reside in Glendale, Arizona where he teaches weekly at a home-based Bible fellowship. He teaches regularly at Desert Winds Retirement Center as well as the Phoenix Rescue Mission. He also accepts invitations to teach at various venues including camps and conferences. He has two children and two grandchildren.

To leave a comment about this book, or to order quantities of this book for your Church or organization, simply use the "Contact" tab on his blog: www.ConfidenceandJoy.com

Made in the USA
Middletown, DE
07 October 2022